42nd Street

Wisconsin/Warner Bros. Screenplay Series

42nd Street

Edited with an introduction by

Rocco Fumento

Published for the Wisconsin Center for Film and Theater Research by
The University of Wisconsin Press

Published 1980

The University of Wisconsin Press
114 North Murray Street
Madison, Wisconsin 53715

The University of Wisconsin Press, Ltd.
1 Gower Street
London WC1E 6HA, England

First printing

Printed in the United States of America

For LC CIP information see the colophon

ISBN 0-299-08100-1 cloth; 0-299-08104-4 paper

Publication of this volume has been assisted by a grant from
The Brittingham Fund, Inc.

Contents

Foreword

In donating the Warner Film Library to the Wisconsin Center for Film and Theater Research in 1969, along with the RKO and Monogram film libraries and UA corporate records, United Artists created a truly great resource for the study of American film. Acquired by United Artists in 1957, during a period when the major studios sold off their films for use on television, the Warner library is by far the richest portion of the gift, containing eight hundred sound features, fifteen hundred short subjects, nineteen thousand still negatives, legal files, and press books, in addition to screenplays for the bulk of the Warner Brothers product from 1930 to 1950. For the purposes of this project, the company has granted the Center whatever publication rights it holds to the Warner films. In so doing, UA has provided the Center another opportunity to advance the cause of film scholarship.

Our goal in publishing these Warner Brothers screenplays is to explicate the art of screenwriting during the thirties and forties, the so-called Golden Age of Hollywood. In preparing a critical introduction and annotating the screenplay, the editor of each volume is asked to cover such topics as the development of the screenplay from its source to the final shooting script, differences between the final shooting script and the release print, production information, exploitation and critical reception of the film, its historical importance, its directorial style, and its position within the genre. He is also encouraged to go beyond these guidelines to incorporate supplemental information concerning the studio system of motion picture production.

We could set such an ambitious goal because of the richness of the script files in the Warner Film Library. For many film titles, the files might contain the property (novel, play, short story, or original story idea), research materials, variant drafts of scripts (from story outline to treatment to shooting script), post-production items such as press books and dialogue continuities, and legal records (details of the acquisition of the property, copyright registration, and contracts with actors and directors). Editors of the Wisconsin/Warner Bros. Screenplay Series receive copies of all the materials, along with prints of the films (the most authoritative ones available for reference purposes), to use in preparing the introductions and annotating the final shooting scripts.

In the process of preparing the screenplays for publication, typographical errors were corrected, punctuation and capitalization were modernized, and the format was redesigned to facilitate readability.

Unless otherwise specified, the photographs are frame enlargements taken from a 35-mm print of the film provided by United Artists.

In 1977 Warner Brothers donated the company's production records and distribution records to the University of Southern California and Princeton University, respectively. These materials are now available to researchers and complement the contents of the Warner Film Library donated to the Center by United Artists.

Tino Balio
General Editor

Introduction
From Bastards and Bitches to Heroes and Heroines

Rocco Fumento

English-born-and-bred Julian Marsh, now a talented and wealthy Broadway impresario, is putting on a new musical entitled *Pretty Lady*. Billy Lawler, despised juvenile lead of the musical, is Marsh's lover. Lawler knows that Marsh is partial to blond chorus boys and has used his influence to have several of them fired. Aging Dorothy Brock—self-centered, vulgar, sluttish—is the star of the show. Pat Denning—weak, shallow, charming— is a gigolo. Currently Denning is hopping from Brock's bed to that of Amy Lee, wife of Andy Lee, the dance director of *Pretty Lady*. Andy, a lecher, hates his wife but cannot leave her because she is blackmailing him. She has proof that he has seduced a nymphet and threatens to hand him over to the authorities. Andy's current mistress is a gold-digging chorine named Lorraine. Young, naïve, syrupy-sweet New Englander Peggy Sawyer comes to New York to conquer Broadway and lands in the chorus of *Pretty Lady*. A shrewish backstage mother, Mrs. Blair, has a bratty teen-age daughter who is an acrobatic specialty dancer. Mrs. Blair encourages her daughter to play up to any man who can further her career. Ex-vaudeville comic Dan Moran lands a role in *Pretty Lady*; Daisy, his simpering, self-pitying partner-wife, does not. Through Marsh's intervention, gangsters try to break up the love affair between Brock and Denning so that Brock will devote herself entirely to *Pretty Lady*'s jealous angel, Dick Endicott. While drunk, Brock falls

9

down a flight of stairs and suffers a concussion. She cannot, of course, go on with the show. Marsh doesn't give a damn about Brock's concussion, but he does give a damn about his show. Lawler sees star quality in Peggy Sawyer, who is being pursued by lecherous chorus boy Terry. To further his own career and to strengthen his hold on Marsh, Lawler suggests Sawyer for the lead. *Pretty Lady* opens with new star Peggy Sawyer. When sweet Peggy realizes that she has created a sensation on stage, she suddenly becomes demanding and bitchy. Amy Lee agrees to leave her husband in exchange for a vast sum of money; she buys Denning's services and together they go off to Paris. Comic Dan Moran, now that he has made it on Broadway, decides that he has outgrown his wife and leaves her. Julian Marsh, with another smash hit on his hands, can still afford to keep Billy Lawler in the style to which he has become accustomed.

The above is a summary of the multiple-plot Bradford Ropes novel *42nd Street*. Such material was not the stuff that American musicals were made of in 1933, not even with the censors napping, not even on the more permissive Broadway stage, at least not until seven years later when that tough, cynical, worldly wise Rodgers and Hart musical, *Pal Joey*, first shocked theater audiences. Based on a story by the then antiromantic John O'Hara, it has as hero a heel who uses his sex appeal to purchase favors from a wealthy older woman. *Pal Joey* was too vinegary for American audiences accustomed to the sweets of a *Sunny*, a *Sally*, or a *Rio Rita*. A musical could be a wee bit naughty (*Whoopee*) if its hero was an eye-popping, Candide-like character played by Eddie Cantor, and a musical could even deal with such controversial subjects as miscegenation (*Show Boat*) if handled in a romantic, melodramatic, tear-jerking manner and if its female lead was a sweet, decent girl named Magnolia. But in 1940, *Pal Joey* was too abrasive for American tastes. Not until a dozen years later, in the cynical climate of post-World War II, did *Pal Joey* at last find an audience. And it was much later that Hollywood brought an equally abrasive musical, *Cabaret*, to the screen.

If the movie version of *42nd Street* had been as frank and as gritty as the novel, it would have been a genuine first for American musicals. The novel is too busy and certainly some of the subplots, those dealing with the Blairs and the Morans, could have been omitted. Yet a daring, but honest, movie based on the novel *could* have been made back in those days, before Mae West awakened the censors with her second film, *She Done Him Wrong*, and with such lines as "Are you packin' a rod or are you just glad to see me?" Of course the censors were around long before Mae West came to Hollywood. And she was not the only target of the 1934 breed of moralists.

Official censorship first came to Hollywood in 1922, after a series of scandals that made the headlines and brought the film business to the attention of the U.S. Congress. To avoid federal censorship, the film industry decided to be its own watchdog. As its white knight and master, the industry chose Will H. Hays to be president of the Motion Picture Producers and Distributors of America, which came to be known as the Hays Office. Hays seemed the perfect choice. He was a Presbyterian elder, he was postmaster general of the United States, he had been President Harding's campaign manager, and he was a nonsmoker, a teetotaler, and a conservative small-town boy from the conservative state of Indiana. The Hays Office's first list of thou-shalt-nots was published in 1927; in 1930 the list was recast into what came to be known as the Production Code. But the Hays Office did little to enforce its Code until, in 1934, it was forced to do so by a public outcry, spearheaded by the newly formed Catholic Legion of Decency, against excessive violence and sex in films. Joseph Breen, a Catholic layman, was hired by the Hays Office to be the stern enforcer of the Code.

But there was no Breen when *42nd Street* was made and released. In such films as *Red Dust, A Free Soul, Rain, Little Caesar, The Public Enemy,* and *Scarface,* Hollywood did not shy away from either sex or violence. Like the prostitute with a heart of gold, *42nd Street* is tough on the outside and soft on the inside. It is a good film that could have been better if Warners had dared to stick more closely to Bradford Ropes's novel.

Not that the Ropes novel is a great novel. It is, in fact, a bad one. The characters are either stereotypes (Dorothy Brock, the aging, bitchy Broadway star) or caricatures (Mrs. Blair, the stridently ambitious backstage mother) or merely flat (the sunshine girl, Peggy Sawyer—at least until her sudden and unconvincing conversion to bitchdom at the very end). The narrative is filled with cliché expressions: "Her heart filled with an almost insupportable pain"; "at this stage of the game"; "a cloak of icy indifference"; "she was a raging hellcat." The prose is bad nineteenth-century Victorian or early twentieth-century O. Henry: "There were feet that moved mechanically, fed by some unquenchable force which overcame the tasks imposed upon them"; "The duties of a producer are manifold as the stars of heaven"; "An agent holds some mesmeric power over the mightiest of Broadway's lords. Though time presses ever so fiercely they will spare a moment to look at some new protege—all protest to the contrary"; "But the machine could not pause to brood over the destinies of the human beings that were caught up in its motion. Machines are impersonal things not given to introspect and retrospect. All that driving force was pounding relentlessly toward one goal—a successful premiere on Forty-Second Street."

Ropes's pages are filled with ludicrous verbs of saying: "carolled the agent," "she piped," "Polly blubbered," "Flo demurred," "she groaned," "Mrs. Blair screeched," "he snapped," "he wheedled," "he whined," "he wailed." And, the plots and subplots to the contrary, the novel is as daring as the swimsuit of a Mack Sennett bathing beauty. Except for a few "goddamns," "bitches," and "bastards," the language is as clean as Dickens's *Christmas Carol*. The novel has no overt sex, no bedroom scenes, and no kiss more ardent than a friendly peck on the cheek in a well-lighted railroad station. Sex cannot improve a good novel, but it can prevent the reader of a bad one from falling asleep. And, in the end, that is what is basically wrong with Bradford Ropes's novel: It is a deadly, sleep-inducing bore.

The novel comes alive only in the hard-as-nails, off-color, often amusing wisecracks. In speaking of his sluttish star, Dorothy Brock, Julian Marsh says, "The only suggestion I have is to take her to some veterinarian and have her spaded [*sic*]." A chorus girl says of one of the snobbish show girls (in Ropes's novel, a show girl has more prestige than a chorus girl), "She's just a good mattress for some tired business man." A chorus girl, referring to another show girl, says, "She's just one of Broadway's whoreified girls" (an obvious play on Ziegfeld's Glorified Girls), "She thinks she's the Broadway lily—and of course you an' me know that dame's slept in more beds than George Washington ever did," and "The wages of sin are generally $99.50 per week—and up." Two chorus girls have this exchange: "I hear old Lily Lowbottom, Andy Lee's girlfriend, ran around with Hughes for a while." "Yeah? When was this?" "Oh, about five abortions ago." None of these wisecracks is in the film. Just one such line from the novel is recognizable in the film. A gossipy, homosexual chorus boy says, "Sophie only said no once an' then she didn't understand what the man asked her." In the film, Andy Lee offers a more compact and cutting version: "She only said no once, and then she didn't hear the question!"

If the novel is so bad, why did Warners want to make a movie of it? Hollywood has always bought bad novels—and many of them reached the screen. For every *Farewell to Arms* there was a *Stella Dallas* and a *Susan Lenox—Her Fall and Rise* and a *White Sister* and, more recently, a *Peyton Place*, a *Where Love Has Gone*, and an *Oliver's Story*. (The above novels were made, and some of them remade, into major productions with major stars. There were also countless programmers based upon novels worse than those mentioned.) Hollywood's major concern is not whether a book is good or bad, but whether it can be made into a money-making movie. Art is usually a secondary concern. *Peyton Place* and *Oliver's Story* were at the top of the best-seller lists for months. Hoping that these bad but money-making novels could be transformed into not-so-bad money-making films, with *Peyton Place* Twentieth Century-Fox gambled and won; with *Oliver's Story* Paramount gambled and lost.

The question becomes, Why not make a movie of *42nd Street*? Its title alone would bring in all those starry-eyed youngsters who dreamed of going to New York and to Forty-second Street, perhaps the most glamourous street in the world to starry-eyed youngsters back in 1933. Its multiple-plot story offered variety and the opportunity to use an all-star cast; its backstage setting offered excitement and pretty chorus girls; and if the characters were too tough and the wisecracks too rough, Warners' scriptwriters could soften the toughness and smooth the roughness and still retain enough of both to please the customers without offending them.

Development of the Screenplay

Whitney Bolton wrote the first treatment (the novel condensed into a story of thirty-eight pages) and delivered it to Warner Brothers on August 16, 1932. Over the next four weeks, he and James Seymour turned in three more versions: an outline treatment (or condensed screenplay) and two screenplays. Then Bolton was dropped and Rian James coauthored the third and final screenplay in time to meet a late September–early October shooting schedule. Though Bolton worked on the film the longest, he receives no screen credit. Perhaps he deserved none because it is apparent that he was in trouble from the very beginning.

The major weakness of the Bolton treatment is that it is directionless, and it is directionless because it has no central plot, character, or characters to pull the numerous subplots and characters together. In a prefatory note to his treatment, Bolton states his intentions: "So far as logic, the stretch of story and geographical exactitude will permit it is proposed to confine the action, the dwellings of the characters and their source to 42nd Street, river to river. It also is proposed to have the making of a musical comedy the dominant factor in the story, subordinating the creatures in it and this great machine which maims one and glorifies another, which breaks a heart here and studs another there with pride." The trouble is that Bolton subordinates his "creatures" so much and juggles so many plots that it is impossible to become interested in any characters or their problems. Both the novel and the film revolve mainly around two characters: Julian Marsh (representing the creative side of the footlights) and Peggy Sawyer (representing the interpretive side); their stories are interwoven throughout, touch upon other characters and their stories, then come together at the end when Marsh makes Sawyer a star. In Bolton's treatment, the first half revolves around Julian; in the second half he is almost forgotten, and Peggy Sawyer, a bit player in the first half, suddenly steps into the limelight. Rather than integration we have fragmentation. This flaw would not be fatal if both characters were interesting, but they are not.

In the novel Julian's homosexuality may not make him a more rounded character, but it does make him more human. In the treatment, he is no longer a homosexual; he is merely wealthy, famous, and damnably dull. Oddly enough, Bolton describes Marsh's apartment in much the same way that Ropes does in his novel: "Dissolve to Marsh's apartment. He's just preparing to dine and Old Alice [this is the only time she is mentioned in the narrative; I assume she is his servant] is fussing about the room. It is a room of grace and proportion. From hangings to small objects it shows taste, a taste just a shade too right, too flawless for the decorator to have been fully masculine. This is just a hint, a suggestion." By the first screenplay the apartment has become quite masculine.

In the novel, speaking to Billy Lawler, Peggy says of herself, "I'm a pretty hopeless person at times. Why, if you hadn't dropped into my life I should be one of millions of colorless young ladies who hopes to land a chorus job from season to season!" And in Bolton's treatment she *is* colorless, making one wonder why three men were chasing after her and why anyone would imagine she was "star" material.

While Bolton changes some of Ropes's plots, he doesn't drop any. The biggest change involves the Danny and Daisy story. Daisy is dead (we're not told the cause of her death) as Bolton's story opens. The first time we see Danny he is returning from her funeral. Two friends are consoling him. One says, "We are terribly sorry to hear about Daisy, Danny. Your grief at the funeral parlor broke me up so I couldn't speak to you there." "You were so pathetic my heart broke for you, Danny," the other friend says. Danny accepts their condolences and then says, "Did you catch me at the grave, boys?" Bolton adds, "Danny reads this line sincerely, there is no attempt to be funny, it is only the actor in him overpowering the newly-bereaved husband. Performance means more to him than natural feeling." The scene is meant, I suppose, to be both poignant and wryly amusing; it is merely silly.

Another major change is that Billy Lawler is now Marsh's "protégé," not his lover, and he does not appear until page 33 of the thirty-eight-page treatment. But when he *does* appear he becomes a major figure since it is he who "discovers" Peggy Sawyer and pushes her toward stardom. Then, nobly, he gives her up: "Good-bye, Peggy. You're on the brink of fame, whatever that means, and God help you if you're not good. Speak to me one of these days when you see me backstage. I'm the fellow they call the juvenile." Bolton's treatment ends with Peggy's being a smash hit and then, as she looks into her dressing room mirror, saying to her reflection, "Darling, if you had any sense you'd go right back to New Jersey and stay there."

Bolton has softened all of the characters somewhat, but basically they are still bastards and bitches. After her opening night triumph, swollen-headed Peggy says to the stage manager, "When you see Phillips [her leading man], tell him not to rush that first chorus. Who does he think he is?" Pat Denning momentarily believes he will reform because of his love for Peggy and then accepts two thousand dollars from Dorothy as compensation for past services. Dorothy deserts Pat for the rich angel, Dick Endicott, at least temporarily, and she remains self-centered and vile tempered. Andy and Amy Lee are still at each other's throats; pushy Mrs. Blair is still willing to give her daughter away to any man who can further Polly's career. But instead of using any of Ropes's abrasively funny wisecracks, Bolton substitutes his own and they are tame and flat. Ann Lowell (who has yet to become "Anytime Annie") says to Jerry, the piano player, as he hands her the lyrics to a new song, "What are these, Mother Goose rhymes?" Jerry says, "Me, I play 'em and like it. You sing 'em and like it!" "I'll sing 'em, darling, but me or the audience either won't like 'em."

From his treatment it was obvious that Bolton needed help, but he needed more than Seymour could give. Together they did a twenty-two-page outline treatment. Everyone is now softer, more decent, except Julian Marsh. We see so little of him that we do not know what he is. The last time he appears he is "immaculate and cool, his show an assured success," so unlike the exhausted and very ill Julian Marsh of the final screenplay and the film. It is apparent that Bolton and Seymour do not know what to do with him. While Marsh's role contracts, Peggy's expands. The major action revolves around her, and instead of becoming a bitch she remains sweet throughout. As a reward she gets Billy Lawler at the end. By this time Ruby Keeler, with a lot of publicity proclaiming that she was a Broadway star *and* the wife of Warners' own Al Jolson, had been chosen to make her movie debut as Peggy.

Some changes in the Bolton-Seymour treatment *are* for the better. The weaker subplots have been eliminated along with such peripheral characters as Dan Moran and his wife, Daisy, and Mrs. Blair and her daughter, Polly. The colorless *Pretty Lady* angel, Dick Endicott, has been dropped, and the comically girl-chasing and older Abner Dillon is the new angel. But where are we in time? We know it is the era of Prohibition and gangsters, but does the action take place before or after the stock market crash? So far there is not a clue.

The first Bolton-Seymour screenplay confirmed the blandness of the story treatment and the outline treatment, as the characters become nicer and the dialogue becomes duller. The lecher Andy Lee is now a harmless comic figure. He no longer has a wife, but his sweetheart (not his mistress) is still Lorraine. Warner Brothers contract players are inked in for various roles. Kay Francis was to play Dorothy Brock, Glenda Farrell was to play Lorraine, and Joan Blondell was to play Ann ("Anytime Annie") Lowell, the roles later taken over by Bebe Daniels, Una Merkel, and Ginger Rogers. Other actors were signed for roles they did play: Dick Powell as Billy Lawler, Edward J. Nugent as Terry, Guy Kibbee as Abner Dillon. Ned Sparks was signed to play Friedman, who becomes Barry in the final. Silent star Henry B. Walthall was signed to play an old actor who dies on stage during dress rehearsal. In this version Julian Marsh finally becomes one of the two pivotal characters and, unlike his behavior in the novel, he is rough on Billy Lawler: "Lawler—you'll never be able to dance—but if you had the brain of a moron you could at least remember the steps!" Also in this version, as in the final, it's a self-sacrificing Ann Lowell and not Billy who pushes Peggy up toward stardom. (It is a weakness of the script and the film that Ann's nobility has no apparent motivation; we see nothing to convince us that Sawyer is a star in the making.)

Someone from above, perhaps production chief Darryl F. Zanuck himself, informed Bolton and Seymour that their first screenplay was not what was expected from a Warner Brothers film. Warner Brothers, which had taught the movies how to talk, was now teaching the movies how not to talk too much. And in this screenplay there was too much talk. It was also too static, too long, and too overdone in character exposition. Bolton and Seymour's second screenplay was a tight 152 pages, 46 pages fewer than their first. Scenes were compressed, or cut, or cut out entirely. The opening four pages are reduced to two and approximate the opening of the final screenplay; the one-page scene with Pat Denning, Peggy, and Peggy's landlady is reduced to half a page; the role of Terry, the chorus boy on the make for Peggy, is cut to half its size.

But the new screenplay is not merely a series of cuts and compressions. There are changes, the most important of which concerns the character of Julian Marsh. Fleshed out, he begins to emerge as a human being with high moods and low moods, outwardly tough and with a wry sense of humor. Instead of being a wealthy ex-Britisher he is now a broke American. "In one pocket—out the other! That's my story," he says. There is still no hint of a Depression in this version. Warners, the producers of films ripped out of the headlines, was perhaps uncertain about how topical a musical ought to be. As in the final version, however, Marsh is recuperating from a nervous breakdown and a doctor warns him that doing another show might kill him. The earlier Bolton-Seymour screenplay is given two endings: The first ends with an embrace between the two young lovers, Peggy and Billy; the second focuses on Marsh who, realizing that *Pretty Lady* is a hit, ignores the congratulations of his backers and, as he walks away, says with a tired shrug, "Just another show!" The ending of the new Bolton-

Seymour screenplay is almost exactly like the James-Seymour final, with Marsh's sitting on the fire escape in the alley and listening to the remarks of the people coming out of the theater as they praise everyone but Marsh himself. "I can't see that Marsh did a thing," one person says. "It's simply having the right cast—that's all!"

Except for the role of Julian Marsh, the "right" cast for the film was now assembled and shooting was to start within a month. In late September, Warner Baxter was borrowed from Fox, for a maximum of six weeks, to play Marsh. His salary was to be $31,200, a tidy sum in those Depression days. But even the second Bolton-Seymour screenplay was not good enough for the so young, so bright, so ambitious ex-scriptwriter-turned-production-chief Darryl F. Zanuck. Bolton was fired and newspaperman Rian James was hired—presumably to do with *42nd Street* what Hecht and MacArthur had done with *The Front Page*. The result was not another *Front Page*; nevertheless, *42nd Street* is a fast and funny show with a few serious moments supplied by the sick and broke Julian Marsh—a character apparently based upon Florenz Ziegfeld, the late, great Broadway impresario who, before his death that same year, was also very sick and very broke.

The major change in the James-Seymour final is in the dialogue. It is slangy, quick paced, and sprinkled liberally with wisecracks. A chorus girl, referring snidely to Ann Lowell, says, "Get Minnie th' Mountaineer!" Ann replies, "It musta been tough on your mother—not having any children." Ann's line has become a cliché; still it's a funnier line than that in the earlier screenplays: "Dry up, you! Unless you want a sock in the ear!" The wisecracks are not as tough as those in the Ropes novel, but at least there *are* wisecracks to liven and lighten the action. One chorus girl to another refers to Billy Lawler and Peggy Sawyer: "Well—if it isn't Little Lord Fauntelroy [*sic*] and the Village Maiden." Second chorus girl laughs: "Made in New York—and all points west!" Or this little exchange between Andy Lee and his girlfriend Lorraine: "Do me a favor—will ya?" he asks. "Not until payday—I won't," she replies.

Some minor changes in the James-Seymour script are incomprehensible: Peggy Sawyer, who originally came from Maine in the novel, subsequently comes from New Jersey, then from Bridgeport, Connecticut, and finally from Sioux City, Iowa. Presumably, Hollywood figured that Sioux City, Iowa, was the closest to being Hicksville, U.S.A. Nor do I understand why Walt McDermott, a smooth, refined, sinister, gangster–speakeasy owner suddenly becomes a cheap hood named Slim Murphy. The cornier scenes (Dorothy on crutches, visiting Peggy backstage, and Marsh's pep talk culminating with "You're going out a youngster—you've *got* to come back a star!") were meant to give the film "heart" and they did, back in those more innocent times of moviemaking and moviegoing.

Even as the film was being made, there were cuts and additions that veer radically from the final. The brothers Warner, as Jack himself admits in his autobiography, were tight with a buck. Therefore we can assume that the scriptwriters were not kept, on the sound stages and on salary, while the film was in progress. We can assume, too, that ex-scriptwriter Zanuck had a hand in the revisions and possibly even director Lloyd Bacon, an old hand at directing fast-paced Warner films. Waring, an actor friend of Pat Denning, is in the final but not in the film. He is not missed and the film is leaner without him. The old actor dying on stage was cut from the film. If his death casts a pall over the *Pretty Lady* company, think what it would do to audiences about to witness the most spectacular musical numbers ever recorded on film! And, let's face it, the scene is even cornier than the two mentioned above. Still, it was best not to back away from reality. The biggest Warner Brothers money-makers were topical, hard-boiled films, gritty with realism. We *were* in the midst of the Great Depression and how could one ignore it in an up-to-the-minute musical about backstage life on "naughty, bawdy, gaudy, sporty, Forty-second Street"?

So in the final, perhaps with a prod from Zanuck, James and Seymour stopped ignoring the Depression. It is referred to twice, first by Dorothy in a scene with Abner Dillon: "Do you know—a year ago, I might have had my choice of a dozen shows—but now with the Depression—" A bit later Marsh refers to it indirectly in an exchange with Jones—Jones: "Say, with all the hits you've had, you ought to be worth plenty." Marsh: "I ought to—but I'm not. Say, did you ever hear of Wall Street?" But these references are made so early in the film that audiences could soon forget about the Depression if they would rather. It was not until later in the year, with *Gold Diggers of 1933* and *Footlight Parade*, that Warners dared to really "look that guy right in the eye" because he (Old Man Depression) had "done us wrong," as Ginger Rogers belts it out in the former film.

Meanwhile other changes, not in the final screenplay, managed to get on film. The opening dissolves are changed to imply strongly that Forty-second Street is the hub of not only numerous intersecting famous streets (Vanderbilt Avenue, Lexington Avenue, Broadway, ultimately spilling into Times Square), but also of New York and, indeed, the entire theater world. More wisecracks are added, most notably Una Merkel's withering comment as, during rehearsal, she's passed from chorus boy to chorus boy: "You've got the busiest hands!" Finally, Ned Sparks's role as Barry is beefed up. In the screenplay Barry is as dull as his partner Jones. But with a first-rate, dead-pan, gravel-voiced comic such as Sparks playing Barry, more lines were thrown his way and the film exploded with some additional laughs.

In late September shooting began; in early November the film was completed at a cost of less than $400,000—not an excessive amount for a big musical, even in those days. Early in January, the film was previewed. It was released to the general public in March, coinciding with the inauguration of Franklin D. Roosevelt as president. Warners, always on the lookout to make a buck or save a buck, hopped on the Roosevelt bandwagon by advertising its film with the slogan Inaugurating a New Deal in Entertainment! An exaggeration yes, but not completely off the mark.

Happy Days Are Here Again!

A musical hailed as the first talkie (*The Jazz Singer*) rescued Warner Brothers from bankruptcy in 1927 and, in the midst of the Great Depression, another musical (*42nd Street*) did the same. So said the sentimental myth-makers of Hollywood. Before *The Jazz Singer*, Warners already had a pair of star money-makers in their two handsome profiles John Barrymore and Rin-Tin-Tin. In those pretalkie days, however, Warners was still a small Hollywood studio and its future was far from bright. It had neither a national distribution system nor access to a steady supply of money to permit the company to grow. How was it possible for this studio to compete with the Big Three, Famous Players–Lasky (later Paramount), Loew's (later MGM), and First National?

It was a man named Waddill Catchings, the head of the investment division of the great Wall Street firm of Goldman, Sachs, who helped to put Warners into the big leagues. Through New York's National Bank of Commerce, Catchings set up a $3 million revolving credit fund. Then he went to the Colony Trust Company of Boston and to four other banks. Through them, Catchings provided Warners with a permanent method of financing future productions. Meanwhile, Warners acquired the Vitagraph Corporation with its nearly fifty exchanges throughout the world, plus two studios, a processing lab, and a film library. With a $4 million debenture issue, Warners established a worldwide distribution system, acquired ten theaters, and was well on its way to competing with the majors. Its final expansionary move led to the coming of sound.

Contrary to popular belief, it was not really *The Jazz Singer* that broke the sound barrier. There had been experimentations with sound almost since film making began. But no studio, with the exception of Warners and Fox, was particularly interested in bringing sound to the screen. Numerous people were working on sound systems, but Warners formed an alliance with Western Electric, and out of this alliance the Vitaphone Corporation emerged. Vitaphone, through contracts with the Victor Talking Machine Company, with the Metropolitan Opera Company, and with individual vaudeville stars, soon had enough talent for the making of short subjects. At about the same time Vitaphone engaged the New York Philharmonic to record background music for the big-budgeted John Barrymore film, *Don Juan*. On August 6, 1926, eight "Vitaphone Preludes" and *Don Juan* opened at the Warner theater in New York. In the following year, on October 6, *The Jazz Singer*, a part-talkie, opened at the same theater and Warners was on its way to the top of the American film industry.

The public's love affair with sound ushered in a boom period for the entire motion picture industry. Between 1928 and 1929 profits from all the studios jumped considerably. But Warners made the biggest leap, with its profits soaring from $2 million to over $4 million. It was time for consolidation, and Warner Brothers, with its early gamble on sound paying off so handsomely, led the way. First it acquired the Stanley Company, which owned a chain of three hundred theaters along the East Coast and a one-third interest in First National. Then it bought out First National's remaining stockholders. In 1925, Warners' assets were a little over $5 million; in 1930 they were valued at $230 million. In only five years Warners had become one of the biggest and most profitable companies in the entire film industry.

By 1933 the Depression had cut moviegoing attendance in half (from 110 million between 1927 and 1930 to 60 million in 1933) and Warners was seriously in debt. Like the other majors, Warners had overextended itself, mainly by having acquired those three hundred theaters. It was impossible for the studio to meet its long-term indebtedness. But the Depression wolf was at every studio's door except MGM's, which was under the protection of Leo the Lion and such formidable box-office stars as Dressler, Beery, Harlow, Gable, Crawford, and Shearer. Warners managed to pacify the wolf, barely, with the films of that tough guy trio of little giants, Edward G. Robinson, James Cagney, and Paul Muni, with such fluke box-office hits as the William Powell–Kay Francis romantic sudser *One Way Passage*, and with the tight-budgeted comedies of loose-mouthed comedian Joe E. Brown. And if the prestige films of Ruth Chatterton and George Arliss erased not one penny of Warners' huge debt, that was the price the studio paid in order to give it some class. They were Warners' answer to MGM's Garbo and Paramount's Dietrich.

Though *42nd Street* was not Warner Brothers' salvation, it was, like Columbia's *It Happened One Night* (1934), a surprise smash hit, a big money-maker, a sleeper that practically no one expected would be a front-runner, a movie that would serve as a model for dozens of subsequent films including Ken Russell's *The Boy Friend* (which tried to satirize it but ended as an exercise in tedium). When *42nd Street* came along, musicals were supposed to be dead. The public had had enough of posturing heroes and prissy heroines, of cramped, smothered-by-sets stagings, of witless dialogue and the preposterous plots of *Dixiana*, *The Vagabond King*, *The Desert Song*, and *Her Majesty, Love*. The only really popular musicals of 1931–32 were *The Big Broadcast*, featuring a large cast of radio stars including Bing Crosby and Kate Smith; the Eddie Cantor vehicles for Samuel Goldwyn, *Palmy Days* and *The Kid from Spain* (both with dances staged by Busby Berkeley); and the intimate, witty, sophisticated boudoir musicals of Ernst Lubitsch (*The Smiling Lieutenant* and *One Hour with You*) and Rouben Mamoulian (*Love Me Tonight*).

John Kobal makes a great deal of sense when he credits much of *42nd Street*'s appeal to the lowly chorus girl: "Once a demure non-participant she now became a predatory calculator, deceptively soft in garters and silk. Her crude, gutsy, and very funny line of repartee made her eminently capable of coping with the wolves and sugar-daddies, swapping fast lines, outsmarting the Babbits and generally casting a caustic look at the world around her. No lost lamb she, quite aware that the best way of keeping the wolf from the door was to coax him inside, where she could fleece him in comfort. Her redeeming virtue (though she was really too much fun to need one) was her tendency to see that the sugar daddies' money went toward financing the show, which would in turn give employment to the entire company of chorines."[1] This is hindsight, however; critics of the day contented themselves mainly with heaping praise (in bad prose) upon Bacon, Berkeley, the performers, and the production in general.

After its sneak preview early in the year, *Variety Bulletin* (January 13, 1933) hailed the movie:

1. John Kobal, *Gotta Sing Gotta Dance: A Pictorial History of Film Musicals* (Feltham, Middlesex, England: Hamlyn House, 1971), p. 112.

As the prelude to a possible cycle of musicals, Warners has given the other studios something to shoot at in *42nd Street*. As received by the preview audiences, it is evident the public is not fed up on musicals if there is a logical reason for tunes and dance routines being inserted in a story.

In *42nd Street* there's a legitimate reason for everything. It's a back stage play, but one of the best that has hit the screen. . . .

Dialog is snappy and of the theatre. Few people of the stage will complain about inaccuracies for there are few, if any. Lloyd Bacon, who knows his theatre, has directed the picture with a great deal of feeling and has held down the histrionics to a minimum. Sparseness of dialog has built up the action and contributed to the picture's speed.

The musical comedy is one of the best so far in a feature. Busby Berkeley's staging is on a high plane, and when the audience in the theatre starts to applaud, there is a reason for it. Not just a flock of chorus girls walking across the stage as a background for the principals, but a suggested story with interesting routines.

When the film was officially released in March, *Variety* (March 14, 1933) held to its earlier evaluation of the film and added:

A money picture for any type of house, and the more cosmopolitan the site the better. Which means it'll be a big grosser. . . .

Furthermore, *42nd Street* looks to be something of a milestone in the field of star making, for Ruby Keeler (Mrs. Al Jolson) is certain marquee timbre. . . .

Miss Keeler . . . is utterly convincing. . . .

Not the least of the total belongs to the direction by Lloyd Bacon, who fashioned some novelties in presentation, with Busby Berkeley an excellent aide on the terp mountings. The same overhead style of camera angles, which Berkeley introduced in the [Eddie] Cantor pictures and elsewhere, are further advanced, manifesting a continued absorption of the cinematographic opportunities. . . .

The songs . . . are primed to fit situations and yet are destined for general favor. *42nd Street* is a nifty lyric which is productioned in corking manner. Camera possibilities here are utilized to the full. . . . The camera goes in for breakaway scenes, dissolves, overhead camera angles and iris-ins and outs that by far exceed what could actually be achieved on a rostrum.

"Shuffle Off to Buffalo" likewise is nifty staging. . . . A honeymoon train breaks apart into a corking effect disclosing compartments, etc., with some nifty production business. Girls here get some special closeup attention, and they're all lookers.

The other trade journals were just as enthusiastic, about both Keeler and the film. *Motion Picture Daily* (February 3, 1933) said:

This is the picture which . . . brings to the public . . . a sweet, demure ingenue with plenty of looks . . . and a pair of gams that know how to step. It wouldn't surprise us a bit if the gang that keeps picture theatres going flops for her in the well known, big way and clamors for more of the looks, plus personality. . . . All of this reminds us that there was never anything wrong with the musical formula any more than there was anything wrong with the gangster film. There were too many rotten ones turned out. . . . A good film, regardless of how you type it, will carve its own niche. The Warner Brothers opus is one of them.

Film Daily (February 3, 1933) ran a signed review by Don Carle Gillettee:

That enterprising Warner organization, which for months has been setting the pace in the production of pictures with a timely pull, delivers again with *42nd Street*. The pioneers in talking pictures, first to smash box-offices with a screen musical comedy, first to set the crowds agog with gangster films, and first in many other production innovations, now lead the way again in the return of musical pictures; and the way they have done it is big news. . . . Dance formations, ensemble routines and trick photography of marvelous cleverness are packed in the last half hour, and the culmination of the heart interest carries a strong punch. Dialogue sometimes is pretty rough, but it's all in fun. In addition to the wreath that is due the Warners for their courage in producing this lavish entertainment, credit goes to Lloyd Bacon for a grand job of directing; to Warner Baxter for a swell performance . . . to Ruby Keeler, as the newcomer who makes good. . . . The success of *42nd Street* will probably bring a new avalanche of musicals.

Mordaunt Hall wrote for the *New York Times* (March 10, 1933):

The liveliest and one of the most tuneful screen musical comedies that has come out of Hollywood was presented last night by the Warner Brothers at the Strand. . . . Although it has its artfully serious moments, it is for the most part a merry affair. . . . It is a film which reveals the forward strides made in this particular medium since the first screen musical features came to Broadway. . . .

This feature begins cleverly and ends without the usual hugging and kissing scene, for which one can be thankful. . . .

The show within the story is imaginatively staged, with clever groupings of dancers and fine photography. . . . It [the "Shuffle off to Buffalo" number] is an excellent example of stagecraft.

The wisecracks are delivered with the necessary flair, and the throng that packed the theatre last night laughed heartily. . . .

There was a time when spectators were satiated with backstage stuff, but here it is pictured brightly and with a degree of authenticity that makes it diverting.

Newspapers ran ads with flattering blurbs for *42nd Street* from various big-name show business personalities. The Warner Brothers press book claims that these "great personalities stepped forward after the preview to label *42nd Street* one of the great attractions of all time." From Jack Pearl: "A picture to rave about!"; from Paul Whiteman: "A really great musical!"; from Bing Crosby: "Something original at last!"; from Kate Smith: "A grand show!"

A few critics complained that because Busby Berkeley's production numbers might be squeezed into Yankee Stadium but not within the tight confines of any Broadway stage they were not realistic. Berkeley had years of stage experience before he ever went to Hollywood. Apparently these critics never stopped to think that Berkeley was the first to know that his numbers could not be performed on any "real" stage. It is their very liberation from the stage that makes them exciting. From the real, stage-bound world of the rehearsal hall, he plunges us into a fantasy world with no boundaries. His chorus boys and girls are performing for the mobile camera, not for the critic anchored in a third row aisle seat. And the camera takes us where Berkeley wants it to take us, from a gigantic close-up of one gorgeous girl to a kaleidoscopic overhead shot of fifty gorgeous girls.

The press agents hailed *42nd Street* as the *Grand Hotel* of musicals. *Grand Hotel* was an all-star MGM indoor epic that had won the Academy Award as best picture for 1932. But *42nd Street* was no *Grand Hotel*. The latter starred MGM's really big guns: Garbo, Crawford, Beery, and both John and Lionel Barrymore. The former had only one major star, Warner Baxter, and even he was not in the same league as that powerhouse five. The look, the styles of both films are quite different. In those days each major studio had its own look, its own style. MGM was noted for its glossy, lush production values and for sets and costumes (by Adrian) that were lavish, sometimes to the point of being vulgar. More often than not its subject matter was noncontroversial and revolved around the people and values of the upper and middle classes.

Grand Hotel is typical of the best of MGM in the 1930s. It is a ravishing, carefully orchestrated film that, even in a viewing today, makes one aware that it is a five-superstar production mounted with an extravagance worthy of its cast. In contrast, *42nd Street* has the lean, hungry, underlit look of Warners' films of the same era. The cheap, tawdry sets are typically Warner Brothers. Even Dorothy Brock's plush hotel suite in Philadelphia is not very plush. Too often the need to economize showed in Warner films, gaining the studio a reputation for a realism rarely seen in the films of the solvent MGM. This enforced economy more often worked for the studio rather than against it. Warner films became known for the gritty look of realism because their subject matter called for it. From this studio came films about gangsters, prisons, the newspaper profession, and topical matters of social consciousness. Its backstage musicals featured poor, hard-working, and hard-boiled chorus girls living in sleazy rooming houses and wearing what looked like off-the-rack clothes. Even the musical numbers of *42nd Street* are not expensively mounted. In fact the "Young and Healthy" number has a lot of chorus boys and girls but no setting whatsoever except for three revolving platforms. To say that *Grand Hotel* is extravagantly mounted and *42nd Street* is not does not mean that the former film is the superior one. It is simply that, despite those press agents' claims, there is no basis for comparison between the two. Both are multiple-plot films and that is all they have in common.

In 1933 there was no such thing as tne soft sell, especially when it came to selling films and when the studio was Warner Brothers. With MGM a discreet "Garbo talks in *Anna Christie*" or

"Garbo laughs in *Ninotchka*" was thought sufficient to sell both films to the public. The idea of Garbo's talking *or* laughing was, I suppose, deemed provocative enough to draw in the crowds. Admittedly, even MGM could get carried away, especially when it came to exploiting a torrid Gable-Harlow picture. Leaping out of the fan magazines is the ad for *Red Dust* (1932) with Gable and Harlow in a passionate embrace and next to them the words "Together! They were born to love! The Flaming Lovers of the Screen, in a Tempestuous Drama of Primitive Passions and Adventure!" But when it came to real purple prose, nobody could top Warners: "Lips of Thunder on Lips of Fire! Love Swept Them to the Desperate Destiny of Those Who Play Against the Rules! A Combination the Devil Himself Couldn't Top! The Irresistible Woman Meets the Immovable Man! IMAGINE . . . the Clash, the Drama, the EXPLOSION when she whispers at last that she loves him . . . AND MANY OTHER MEN!" So read the ad for *I Loved a Woman* starring Edward G. Robinson and Kay Francis. Those were the days when ads were fun—and filled with wild exaggerations and downright lies.

The January previews of *42nd Street* convinced Warners that it had a hit on its hands, and the press agents and admen pulled out all the stops in anticipation of the general release of the film in March and in response to the studio's dictum (as recorded in the film's ad campaign, sent out to exhibitors) to "Sell '42nd Street' as Biggest Screen Event since Birth of Vitaphone." Under this bannerline the hard sell really begins: "No picture since Warner Brothers turned the show world upside down with *The Jazz Singer* has meant more to film business than *42nd Street*. Musical entertainment comes back to the screen, not merely as an improvement over the old, but as something vastly different and sensationally new. *42nd Street* is a show which must be sold with direct and forceful campaigning." The directive goes on and on suggesting ways to publicize the film: by conducting look-alike contests of the stars; by serializing the story, with scenes from the film, in the local newspapers; by flooding the newspapers with material about the stars and the production: "He [Busby Berkeley] Scanned 5,000 to Find 150 Chorines,"

"Ruby Keeler Timid When Meeting Film Stars," "Hollywood Stars Anxious for George Brent as Leading Man," and so forth, and so forth.

"This ad ran in the March issue of nine leading magazines reaching more than 11,812,760 people. A special enlargement, 44 by 64 in two colors, red and dark blue, has been made available for your use. Use it as an advance frame with a date line and currently with your run. At your exchange for only 50 cents each! Take advantage." So ran the advance copy sent out to exhibitors, and the exhibitors bought the two-color blowups. The ad, the one most associated with the film, is first-class Warner Brothers schlock (see figure 1). Nothing is omitted except Busby Berkeley's name as director of production numbers; in ads for future Warner musicals there was never again such an oversight. The ad claims that the film has fourteen stars. The only real star was Warner Baxter. Bebe Daniels had been a star throughout the twenties and into the very early thirties, but by 1933 her luster was fading and by 1935 she was through in Hollywood, though she subsequently, along with her husband, Ben Lyon, became a radio and then a television star in England. In 1933 George Brent was known more as Ruth Chatterton's husband and sometime leading man than as an actor, and he was certainly not a star. Ruby Keeler would achieve stardom, but she was not a star in this film. Una Merkel was and remained a dependable supporting actress; Dick Powell was still a juvenile lead, not a star; later in the year Ginger Rogers, along with Fred Astaire, would achieve stardom, but in *42nd Street* she was not there yet. Guy Kibbee, Ned Sparks, George E. Stone, Eddie Nugent, Allen Jenkins, and Robert McWade were and remained talented supporting actors and/or comedians. Henry B. Walthall had been a star in silent films from the time he played the role of "The Little Colonel" opposite Lillian Gish in D. W. Griffith's *Birth of a Nation* (1915), but by the time he made *42nd Street* he was playing supporting roles. It was an insult to Walthall, and to any following he might still have had, to list him as one of the film's stars. He was to play the role of the old actor who dies on stage, but that scene was cut out of the film and he was reduced to playing a nonspeaking bit role.

Introduction

Despite all the hyperbole, *42nd Street* remains a watershed film, a highly entertaining musical peppered with Lloyd Bacon's bullet-paced (a taut eighty-nine minutes) direction; some good ensemble acting, particularly from those handling the comic lines: Guy Kibbee, Una Merkel, Ginger Rogers, Ned Sparks, and George E. Stone; some lively songs by Al Dubin and Harry Warren; and the exuberant excesses of a young Busby Berkeley.

Backstage

In the ads for *42nd Street* Busby Berkeley, unlike director Lloyd Bacon, received no billing. Ironically, he was the real overnight star of the film, not Ruby Keeler. Keeler lived up to Warners' expectations; Berkeley exceeded them. Columnist Jimmy Starr in the *New York Herald Express* said, "*42nd Street* is a cinematic effort by which Busby Berkeley, and he alone, is responsible for the current return of celluloid musicals." [2] This may have been an overstatement; nevertheless, after *42nd Street*, Warner musicals with production numbers by Berkeley were referred to as Busby Berkeley films although, usually, the films themselves were directed by others, most often by Bacon. Berkeley, who wanted desperately to be a director, was allowed to direct a number of films, mostly nonmusicals, all without distinction except for *They Made Me a Criminal*, which starred John Garfield. It wasn't until he left Warners, in 1939, that he directed some good musicals, most notably the series of Judy Garland–Mickey Rooney films for MCM beginning with *Babes in Arms*.

Berkeley had been in Hollywood for several years before he made *42nd Street*. He was hired by Samuel Goldwyn to stage the production numbers for Eddie Cantor's *Whoopee* (1930). He was dance director for eight pictures (including several others for Goldwyn-Cantor), without anyone's really noticing, before he moved over to Warners as dance director for *42nd Street*.

Berkeley began as an actor on the stage, mainly in stock companies but sometimes on Broadway. But he wanted to direct, and for nearly six years he directed nonmusical plays in stock

2. Quoted in Tony Thomas and Jim Terry (with Busby Berkeley), *The Busby Berkeley Book* (Greenwich, Conn.: New York Graphic Society, 1973), p. 54.

companies all over the East Coast. He was pushed into a musical, both directing and acting, against his will. In his words,

We put on the show; and it ran for a week; and we followed it with a dramatic show. About ten weeks later they came to me again and wanted to do another musical. I said, "Let me out!"

But they countered with, "We thought we heard you say you'd do it all yourself." Then they said, "But you don't dance!"

I told them, "I can do what those dames did! All they did was kick their feet up in the air." So I put on the show; and it ran for four weeks—something unheard of in stock. Word got around, and other stock companies throughout the East . . . started to write to me and wire me and phone to see if I wouldn't come to their cities and put on a musical.[3]

That was how it all began for the man who "never took a dancing lesson in my life." What he learned about dancing, he admits, he learned from observing chorus girls.

Berkeley, the nondancer, rarely directed *dance* numbers. In some of his biggest production numbers there is either no dancing whatsoever or very little: "Young and Healthy" and "Shuffle off to Buffalo" from *42nd Street*; "Remember My Forgotten Man" and "Pettin' in the Park" from *Gold Diggers of 1933*; "By a Waterfall," "Sitting on a Backyard Fence," and "Honeymoon Hotel" from *Footlight Parade*; "The Girl at the Ironing Board" and the "Dames" number from *Dames*, and many others.

Instead of dancing, what Berkeley gives us is movement: girls forming snakelike, phallic patterns either on solid ground ("Young and Healthy") or in water ("By a Waterfall"); chorus boys and girls marching in military fashion ("Shanghai Lil" from *Footlight Parade* and "All's Fair in Love and War" from *Gold Diggers of 1937*); girls bending their bodies to form human harps, which other girls are strumming ("Spin a Little Web of Dreams" from *Fashions of 1934*); girls seated at baby grands as the baby grands form intricate patterns ("The Words Are in My Heart" from *Gold Diggers of 1935*); girls with scores of normal-sized

3. Bob Pike and Dave Martin, *The Genius of Busby Berkeley* (Reseda, Calif.: Creative Film Society Books, 1973), p. 25.

neon-lit violins forming one giant neon-lit violin ("Shadow Waltz" from *Gold Diggers of 1933*); girls with boards on their backs fitting them together to form a gigantic jigsaw puzzle of Ruby Keeler's face in *Dames*. The girls move, the camera moves, baby grands glide across the floor, the floors revolve, and all combine to form astonishing kaleidoscopic patterns. Audiences were dazzled and the name Busby Berkeley entered the lexicon of film.

With all the razzle-dazzle surrounding Berkeley, one is apt to forget Lloyd Bacon's contribution to *42nd Street*. Bacon had been in films since the end of World War I, first as an actor and then, beginning in 1926, as a director. From 1926 through 1954 he directed ninety-eight films. Stanley Kubrick has been making films since 1953. He has made eleven films. One cannot, of course, measure a movie's worth by the yard and, undoubtedly, critics would agree that none of Bacon's films is as good as most of Kubrick's. Yet I wonder if any of today's directors could maintain the high level of competency, especially under strong studio control, that Bacon maintained in a shade less than thirty years—directing movies in almost every genre, directing Warners' eternally battling top star, James Cagney, in fourteen films and the equally combative Bette Davis in several, directing a score of other major, and often difficult, stars including Edward G. Robinson, Kay Francis, Errol Flynn, Humphrey Bogart, Loretta Young, and Clark Gable. No one can call Bacon an auteur, but he rarely directed a dull film, and he directed some that one still remembers with affection and respect: *A Slight Case of Murder, Marked Woman, Footlight Parade, Brother Orchid, Boy Meets Girl,* and *Action in the North Atlantic.*

The title of the last-named tells us a great deal about Bacon and about the way he saw himself. In an interview with William R. Meyer Bacon said, "I see that the public gets action. Some others may use motion pictures as a vehicle for a psychological study. I haven't that patience." Meyer credits Bacon with a great deal of the success of *42nd Street*: "It was Lloyd who kept up human interest in the film between Berkeley's dazzling production numbers. The greatness of *42nd Street* is its unity of drama, music, and comedy. The film simply wouldn't be the same without even one of these elements, and the classic musical's characters could not possibly have convincingly brought the narrative to its poignant conclusion without the firm, calm hand of Lloyd Bacon."[4]

Bacon may not have had the patience to make "psychological" movies, but certainly he must have used patience and psychology to work smoothly with a large, edgy cast in *42nd Street*. Warner Baxter, though still very much a popular favorite, had not had a major hit since the 1931 *Daddy Long Legs*; Bebe Daniels was frantically trying to revive a faltering career; Ruby Keeler was a nervous ingenue making her film debut; featured players Ginger Rogers, Dick Powell, George Brent, and Una Merkel were all desperately reaching for the brass ring of stardom; former star Henry B. Walthall, uneasy in talkies, was trying for a new career as a character actor. Bacon completed the film in less than six weeks, with all egos intact, giving Baxter the major hit he needed, helping to prolong Daniels's career by a couple of years, easing Keeler into stardom, and boosting the careers of soon-to-be stars Rogers, Powell, and Brent. Perhaps it was his ability to work easily with even the most difficult actors, coupled with his ability to make good movies rapidly, that made him "Jack's [Warner] favorite" and, during the thirties, the studio's "highest paid director, at $4,225 a week."[5] At the same time Busby Berkeley was making $1,750 a week.

The weakest, yet paradoxically the strongest, link in the chain of Warner Brothers musicals of the thirties is the team of Ruby Keeler and Dick Powell. (They made seven films together.) One wonders why they were so popular. When Keeler sings one imagines there's something wrong with the sound track; when she dances, she's a klutz; when she acts, she runs the gamut of two expressions: a blissful smile, a worried frown. As for Powell, he simply grins his way cheerfully throughout these musicals. And if his singing is better than Keeler's, his dancing is worse.

Yet there is no doubt that they charmed people. I am charmed

4. William R. Meyer, *Warner Brothers Directors* (New Rochelle, N.Y.: Arlington House, 1978), p. 15.

5. James R. Silke, *Here's Looking at You, Kid* (Boston: Little, Brown, 1976), p. 144.

by Keeler even as I see her old films over and over again. There's something so very vulnerable about her, so moronically endearing in her klutziness while she earnestly looks down at her feet as she clumps her way up Forty-second Street. As a tap dancer, certainly she was no Eleanor Powell or Ann Miller or, ironically enough, no Ginger Rogers, who gives up a chance at stardom to give that "talented youngster" a break. But women liked her; she was much too nice to steal a husband or a sweetheart away. Older men wanted to protect her (and her incredible innocence) from the cruel, cynical world; younger men wanted to embrace her and make her their wife, *never* their mistress; and to boys stumbling into puberty she was an angel, a first infatuation, a dream girl bigger and better than life up there on that silver screen—a madonna of the musicals.

Keeler's contract with Warners terminated in 1937 and she left the studio supposedly to retire. But in 1938 she accepted a non-musical role in RKO's *Mother Carey's Chickens*, a role that Katherine Hepburn had wisely refused. Keeler's last film, except for a cameo role in the *The Phynx* in 1970, was a B musical made in 1941 and called *Sweetheart of the Campus*. At the time she was almost old enough to be a housemother and certainly too old to be a campus cutie. In 1970 she and Busby Berkeley worked together again in the stage revival of *No, No, Nanette*, and once again, with no more talent than she had ever possessed, she charmed an enchanted public.

Next to Crosby, Powell was the great crooning heartthrob throughout the thirties. At the same time older women warmed up to him because he was so much "like that nice boy next door." By the early forties Powell's career was in decline. He fought to destroy the image of the old singing, smiling Powell. After all, he was no longer a juvenile. In 1944 he succeeded in destroying that image when he landed the role of Philip Marlowe in *Murder, My Sweet*, the first film version of Raymond Chandler's *Farewell, My Lovely*. In the mid-fifties he turned to directing, and in the late fifties he broke into television and made millions as a performer, director, and producer before his death in 1963.

Though Warner Baxter plays a harried impresario in *42nd*

Street, it was his role as the carefree, debonair Cisco Kid in his first talkie, *In Old Arizona* (1929), that won him an Academy Award. Baxter had been making films since 1914 and, by the late twenties, was inching his way toward stardom in such films as *The Great Gatsby* and *Ramona*. But it was *In Old Arizona* that made him a true star, and he remained one for the next decade. In the forties he was reduced to playing leads in B films, mainly in the Crime Doctor series, but he worked steadily and profitably until 1950, the year before his death. Ginger Rogers, after dancing her way through a series of classic RKO musicals opposite Fred Astaire, won an Academy Award for a dramatic role in *Kitty Foyle* (1940). George Brent, though his career spanned a period of twenty-two years, never achieved top stardom. Like Herbert Marshall, he was the perfect, self-effacing leading man for such female superstars as Garbo, Myrna Loy, Bette Davis, Barbara Stanwyck, Claudette Colbert, Olivia de Havilland, Joan Fontaine, Kay Francis, and Hedy Lamarr. Una Merkel, who never became a star, made a career out of playing bubble-headed blondes until she startled her fans by giving a sensitive dramatic performance as Geraldine Page's mother in Tennessee Williams's *Summer and Smoke* (1962).

Some credit for *42nd Street*'s success, particularly in the production numbers, belongs to cinematographer Sol Polito. In order to get one of the overhead kaleidoscopic shots, he and Berkeley rode far up into the rafters on Berkeley's "monorail" (actually two rails) invention. Polito's film credits are impressive and varied and include the probing, chiaroscuro cameras of *I Am a Fugitive from a Chain Gang* and *The Sea Wolf*, the radiant, sun-drenched color cameras of *The Adventures of Robin Hood*, and the tension-building, nervously cross-cutting cameras of *Sorry, Wrong Number*.

Regrettably, the scriptwriters seem to have contributed the least to the success of *42nd Street*. It's a pity that in dropping the dullness of Bradford Ropes's novel, Rian James, James Seymour, and Whitney Bolton also dropped the daring. Al Dubin's lyrics to the title song capture more of the excitement of a legendary Forty-second Street than do the various screenplays.

Where are all those indiscreet sexy ladies from the eighties and why don't we see the underworld meeting the elite? They played it safe, those scriptwriters—or perhaps they were ordered to play it safe. Still, it is the rare screenplay that can stand squarely on its own merits.[6] Consider what *Casablanca* would be without Bogart, Bergman, and a marvelous supporting cast, without the highly charged atmosphere created by Arthur Edeson's camera and Michael Curtiz's direction, and without Dooley Wilson caressing the piano keys and breaking our hearts with "As Time Goes By."

6. On December 5, 1979, *Variety* announced that "David Merrick is proceeding with plans for a Broadway musical version of *42nd Street*, the 1933 Warner Bros. film. The show is now aimed for Broadway early next season, after a summer stand at the Kennedy Center, Washington. . . . The production will use the original Harry Warren songs from the film."

BIBLIOGRAPHY

Baxter, John. *Hollywood in the Thirties*. New York: A. S. Barnes, 1968.

Bergman, Andrew. *We're in the Money: Depression America and Its Films*. New York: Harper & Row, 1972.

Cagney, James. *Cagney on Cagney*. New York: Doubleday, 1976.

Fortune. "The Hays Office." In *The American Film Industry*, edited by Tino Balio, pp. 295–314. Madison: University of Wisconsin Press, 1976.

Gomery, J. Douglas. "The Coming of the Talkies." In *The American Film Industry*, edited by Tino Balio, pp. 193–211. Madison: University of Wisconsin Press, 1976.

Griffith, Richard, and Mayer, Arthur. *The Movies*. New York: Simon & Schuster, 1970.

Kobal, John. *Gotta Sing Gotta Dance: A Pictorial History of Film Musicals*. Feltham, Middlesex, England: Hamlyn House, 1971.

Mast, Gerald. *A Short History of the Movies*. Second Edition. Indianapolis: Bobbs-Merrill, 1976.

Meyer, William R. *Warner Brothers Directors*. New Rochelle, N.Y.: Arlington House, 1978.

Pike, Bob, and Martin, Dave. *The Genius of Busby Berkeley*. Reseda, Calif.: Creative Film Society Books, 1973.

Sennett, Ted. *Warner Brothers Presents*. Secaucus, N.J.: Castle Books, 1971.

Silke, James R. *Here's Looking at You, Kid*. Boston: Little, Brown, 1976.

Sweeney, Russell C. *Coming Next Week: A Pictorial History of Film Advertising*. New York: A. S. Barnes, 1973.

Thomas, Tony, and Terry, Jim (with Busby Berkeley). *The Busby Berkeley Book*. Greenwich, Conn.: New York Graphic Society, 1973.

Warner, Jack (with Dean Jennings). *My First Hundred Years in Hollywood*. New York: Random House, 1964.

1. *Amusing in its outrageous exaggerations, this ad is the one most often associated with the film.*

2. *Films of the 1930s and 1940s typically opened with this kind of establishing shot—an aerial view of Manhattan.*

3. *After this establishing shot, a series of dissolves shows other 42nd Street signs intersecting with Lexington Avenue, Broadway, and, ultimately, Times Square, the glamourous heart of Manhattan's theater district.*

4. *Montage: huge lips in the background and various extras in the foreground, all mouthing the news that "Jones and Barry are doing a show!"*

5. *The back cover of the magazine Bebe Daniels peers over was not advertising Seagram's 7 then. Prohibition was not repealed until several months after the film was completed.*

6. Framed in an office window, Warner Baxter, ill, broke, and alone, swears he's going to put on one last great show even if it kills him.

7. George E. Stone insults Ginger Rogers with a wisecrack: "She only said no once, and then she didn't hear the question!" Una Merkel, his embarrassed girlfriend, looks on.

8. *Ruby Keeler blunders into Dick Powell's dressing room. In a typical 1930s scene, boy meets girl in an embarrassing moment.*

9. *Baxter is the loner—no wife, no sweetheart, no friends. A feeling of aliena-tion is evoked by showing him alone, detached from others, and often with the darkened theater as background.*

10. *During a rehearsal break, Eddie Nugent offers to show Ruby Keeler a new dance step as a jealous Dick Powell looks on.*

11. *Rehearsing the ludicrous "It Must Be June" number. The underlit stage here and the underlit settings elsewhere prompted critics to call the film a "realistic" musical.*

12. *George Brent and Daniels, supposedly in a moving car. Back projection was hard to detect in those days of smaller theater screens and car windows.*

13. *Baxter badgers the weary chorus girls, commands them to pick up the tempo, drives them to dance faster, faster . . .*

14. . . . . *until Ruby Keeler has a fainting spell. Here a sympathetic George Brent revives her in the theater alley.*

15. *Now it's Keeler's turn to be sympathetic. Brent has just been beaten up by thugs and warned to stay away from Daniels.*

16. *Flanked by George E. Stone (left) and Allen Jenkins, Baxter gives the exhausted girls one final peptalk—but more gently this time.*

17. *Brent attempts to calm a drunk, angry, and jealous Daniels, as an anxious Keeler looks on. A few seconds later Daniels falls and sprains her ankle.*

18. *The shabby dressing room is typical Warners economy, yet it is realistic, unlike Joan Crawford's lavish one in MGM's* Dancing Lady *(also 1933).*

19. *Baxter's frantic and often-parodied plea to Keeler just before she debuts as leading lady: "You're going out a youngster—you've got to come back a star!"*

20. *Keeler shuffles off to Buffalo with Clarence Nordstrom in one of Busby Berkeley's "story" production numbers.*

21. *"Matrimony is baloney" to both Una Merkel (with the banana) and Ginger Rogers lounging in an upper berth of the honeymoon special to Buffalo. Freud might have had a field day with this scene.*

22. *Berkeley created a dazzling kaleidoscopic effect with two stages revolving in contrary motion, white against black, and overhead cameras.*

23. *Again "Young and Healthy" is effective with only ribbons for props instead of elaborate sets, with a great deal of movement instead of dancing, and with white against black instead of Technicolor.*

24. *In the "42nd Street" number, the camera pulls back to reveal that Keeler is dancing atop a taxicab.*

25. *Scrambling down from the taxicab, heavy-footed Keeler next clumps her way down Forty-second Street.*

26. *Publicity claimed that almost two hundred girls were in this number; I count about fifty. Again note Berkeley's black and white composition.*

27. *Baxter has another hit, but he's too exhausted to care. It looks as if a bit of German expressionism has crept into this final scene. Certainly it's not a typical ending for a musical comedy.*

42nd Street

Screenplay
by
RIAN JAMES
and
JAMES SEYMOUR

42nd Street

FADE IN

1.   AERIAL SHOT   NEW YORK CITY

concentrating on midtown Manhattan. The shot is taken from a plane that suddenly zooms head on into a street sign reading in CLOSE-UP

42nd Street

RAPID DISSOLVE TO:

2.   STREETCAR SIGN

reading:

42nd Street Crosstown

RAPID DISSOLVE TO:

3.   STREET SIGN

reading:

42nd Street

CAMERA PANS around lamppost to show dual sign reading:

Broadway

and PANS BACK around lamppost to show sign again reading:

42nd Street

RAPID DISSOLVE TO:

4.   FERRY SLIP SIGN

reading:

42nd Street Ferry

RAPID DISSOLVE TO:

5.   BILLBOARD SIGN

reading:

42nd Street Association

RAPID DISSOLVE TO:

6.   RESTAURANT SIGN
     reading:

                 42nd Street Eat Shoppe

                                RAPID DISSOLVE TO:

7.   DOORMAN'S HAT
     the lettering on which reads:
                 42nd Street Building

                                RAPID DISSOLVE TO:

8.   SUBWAY STATION SIGN
     reading:

                 42nd Street—Times Square

                                RAPID DISSOLVE TO:

9.   MED. SHOT   42ND STREET AND BROADWAY
     showing busy, bustling mobs and whirling traffic at
     high speed.

                                RAPID DISSOLVE TO:

10. MARQUEE SIGN
     reading:

                 42nd Street Theater

                                RAPID DISSOLVE TO:

11. STREET SIGN
     reading:

                 42nd Street

                                RAPID DISSOLVE TO:

12. FULL SHOT   42ND STREET BUILDING   WEST OF 7TH
     AVENUE

                                PAN UP SIDE TO:

13. CLOSE SHOT   OFFICE WINDOW
     on second floor with lettering reading:
                 CONROY AND KRANTZ
                   Music Publishers
               Composers of Klassy Klassics

                                DISSOLVE TO:

14.   INT. FULL SHOT   OFFICE
Battered piano, paper-littered desk, and two sweltering, shirt-sleeved men busy with score sheets. One at piano picks out a melody with one finger; other, paper in hand, stands beating out tempo.

TRUCK UP TO:

15.   CLOSE-UP   MUSICAL SCORE SHEET
with penciled notes and corrections. Scrawled across top of page:

PRETTY LADY
Score—Opening Chorus

WIPE OFF TO:

16.   EXT. CLOSE-UP   STREET SIGN
reading:

42nd Street
8th Avenue

PAN TO:

17.   FULL SHOT   CORNER BUSINESS BUILDING
CAMERA PANS up side.

DISSOLVE TO:

18.   EXT. FULL SHOT   AWNINGED PENTHOUSE PATIO
Gorgeous, lightly clad show girl lolls on striped canvas glider couch, watching with vast disinterest tousle-haired youth banging furiously at typewriter.

TRUCK UP TO:

19.   CLOSE-UP   PAGE IN TYPEWRITER
At top is typed: Pretty Lady—Act II—Scene 4. As words of scene are typed in

WIPE OFF TO:

20.   CLOSE-UP   STREET SIGN
reading:

42nd Street
2nd Avenue

PAN UP TO:

21. EXT. FULL SHOT 42ND STREET APARTMENT BUILDINGS
(Tudor City)

DISSOLVE TO:

22. CLOSE SHOT APARTMENT ENTRANCE
with metal plaque reading:
Forty-second Street Towers

DISSOLVE TO:

23. CLOSE-UP THEATRICAL CONTRACT
held in man's pudgy hands.

DISSOLVE TO:

24. CLOSE-UP OPENING PARAGRAPH OF CONTRACT
reading in proper legal phraseology (use genuine Equity
contract, first paragraph):

> Jones and Barry,[1] Theatrical Producers,
> hereby engage *Dorothy Brock* to star in
> their musical production *Pretty Lady* at a
> weekly salary of $1200.00 for run of
> show.

25. INT. MED. SHOT DOROTHY'S LIVING ROOM
Abner Dillon, with contract in hands, stands by Dorothy
Brock, who wears a stunning, sexy tea gown, at table
near windows looking down west along Forty-second
Street toward Broadway. On table are two highballs.

ABNER (walking to table and picking up highball, raising
it almost preparatory to delivering a toast, and beaming
appreciatively):

> Well, I ain't a lawyer, but it sounds like a good
> contract to me.

DOROTHY (a trifle coyly; walking to table and picking up
her own glass):

> Good! It's perfect—thanks to you—MIS-ter Dillon.
> Do you know—a year ago, I might have had my
> choice of a dozen shows—but now with the De-
> pression[2]—well, if it hadn't been for Abner Dil-
> lon, the Kiddie Kar King . . .[3]

ABNER (fatuously; with meaning):
Why Miss Brock—Dorothy—I'd like to—to do a lot for you . . . if . . . if you'd do something for me . . .

DOROTHY (raising her eyebrows quickly and on guard; she turns toward him, coyly twiddling her finger in his heavy watch chain):
Why Mister Dillon—of course—but what could I possibly do for you?

ABNER (fussed, blushing, and awkwardly coy):
Call me—Ab-ner! (In a slow drawl.)

WIPE OFF TO:

26.   EXT. CLOSE-UP   STREET SIGN
reading:
42nd Street
7th Avenue

PAN AROUND TO:

27.   EXT. FULL SHOT   CANDLER BLDG. (220 W. FORTY-SECOND STREET)
CAMERA passing facade "Forty-second Street Theater" (New Amsterdam) as it moves.

DISSOLVE TO:

28.   INT. CLOSE-UP   CONTRACT ON DESK
as man's hand awkwardly scratches signature: A. Jones. Second hand comes into scene and scrawls Thomas Barry, then passes pen to slim manicured fingers, which sign with a suave flourish: Julian Marsh.

TRUCK BACK TO:

29.   FULL SHOT   OFFICE OF "JONES AND BARRY"
Jones and Barry, glowing with satisfaction, regard Julian Marsh, immaculately groomed, almost dandified, as he straightens up and lays aside pen, after signing contract.

BARRY:
We got three good tunes—a coupla swell

blackouts—and Dorothy Brock's—er— (He glances down at a photograph on his desk.)

CAMERA PANS TO:

30. CLOSE-UP OF PHOTOGRAPH
showing Dorothy Brock posed in a short, filmy drape— almost nude—as we hear:

BARRY'S VOICE OFF (continuing):
—big blue eyes. Can you make it a hit show, Julian?

MARSH (dryly):
I've made hit shows out of less!

JONES (a little disparagingly):
Say, with the percentage he's getting, he should be able to make a hit show out of Webster's dictionary.

BARRY:
When we got Dorothy Brock, that was a break. Abner Dillon has guaranteed to finance anything she does.

MARSH (unimpressed):
I'll give you a good show in spite of that. Say, these days, stars like Dorothy Brock are a dime a dozen.

JONES:
That's why we got you, Julian. Julian Marsh—the greatest musical comedy director in America today!

MARSH:
What do you mean—TODAY?

BARRY:
All right—tomorrow, too. Say, with your reputation—

MARSH:
Did you ever try to cash a reputation at a bank? I'm in this for one reason only . . . MONEY!

JONES:
>   Money? *You?* Say, with all the hits you've had, you ought to be worth plenty.

MARSH:
>   I ought to be—but I'm not. Say, did you ever hear of Wall Street? [4]

Girl secretary steps into room.

SECRETARY (to Marsh):
>   Excuse me, Mr. Marsh—there's a phone call for you—a Dr. Chadwick . . .

MARSH (starts and frowns):
>   Er—tell him I'll call him back.

SECRETARY (apologetically):
>   But he says it's urgent—about your examination!

Marsh hesitates. Jones and Barry exchange perturbed looks.

BARRY (indicating phone on his desk):
>   Use our private phone, Julian.

Marsh nods. Secretary exits. Marsh sits down and is about to pick up the telephone receiver but hesitates. Then, looking quickly from Barry to Jones, he frowns, shrugs, and picks up the receiver. Jones and Barry watch him apprehensively.

MARSH (quietly):
>   What is it, Doc?

31.   CLOSE-UP   MARSH AT PHONE

MARSH (listens a moment):
>   You have? (He frowns more deeply, then continues harshly.) Nevertheless, I've just signed the contract
>   . . .

32. CLOSE SHOT   JONES AND BARRY BY DESK
exchange meaning, anxious glances. Jones nervously
fingers contract.

MARSH'S VOICE OFF (impatiently):
Of course I realize . . . I understand perfectly . . .

33. CLOSE-UP   MARSH AT PHONE

MARSH (jaw clenching):
I know—but there's no other way!

34. CLOSE SHOT   DOCTOR AT DESK
He is telephoning. Reports, analysis, etc., are on desk
before him.

DOCTOR (vehement, much wrought up):
. . . but good lord, man . . . you're not a machine
. . . that body of yours will stand just so much . . .
you're not just headed for another nervous breakdown . . . any undue strain on your part might
easily prove fatal.[5]

35. CLOSE-UP   MARSH AT PHONE

MARSH (grimly):
Sorry, Doc, but I'll have to risk it.

He hangs up and starts to rise.

36. FULL SHOT   MARSH, JONES, AND BARRY BY DESK
as Marsh rises.

JONES (excitedly):
Anything wrong, Julian?

Marsh, busy lighting cigarette, does not reply.

BARRY (apprehensively):
You ain't gonna have another breakdown?

JONES (quickly):
If that's what it is—

MARSH (curtly, interrupting):
The contract's signed—isn't it?

BARRY (sharply):
But that don't matter—we can—

MARSH (definitely):
It holds! You'll get your *Pretty Lady!*

He turns on heel, crossing irritably to window.

37.   CLOSE SHOT   MARSH AT WINDOW
his back to room, looking out. CAMERA SHOOTS DOWN
past him, showing busy Forty-second Street in
background. Marsh turns and faces the other two.

MARSH (grimly; raising his hand to stall off any protest):
YOU haven't got anything to worry about. I'm not
going to let you down . . . (he turns to the window
and speaks reflectively over his shoulder, without
looking around) because I can't afford to!

Slowly, he puts his hands deep into his trousers pockets, shrugs, and, continuing to look dreamily out of the
window, continues.

MARSH:
I've given everything I've had to that gulch down
there . . . It's taken all I had to offer . . . It paid me
. . . sure . . . in money I couldn't hang on to . . .
Fair-weather friends . . . women . . . headlines
. . . Why even the cops and newsboys recognize
me on sight . . . Marsh, the Magnificent . . .
Marsh, the slave driver . . . Actors tell you how
Marsh drove 'em . . . bullied 'em . . . (he takes
his hands out of his pockets and unconsciously
clenches his fists) and tore it out of them . . .
(more softly now) and maybe a few'll tell you how
Marsh really made 'em . . . and they all have something to show for it . . . except Marsh! Well, this is
my last shot! I'll make a few more of 'em . . . and

> this time I'll sock my money away so hard they'll
> have to blast to find enough to buy a newspaper!
> THAT'S why I'm going ahead with *Pretty Lady!*

He turns around slowly and walks toward CAMERA.
CAMERA TRUCKS BACK and PANS AROUND, as he crosses
room to get his hat and stick. Jones and Barry, much
perturbed, start toward him.

38.   FULL SHOT   OFFICE

MARSH:
> . . . And *that's* why *Pretty Lady* has GOT to be a hit.
> It's my last show—it's GOT to be my best. You're
> counting on me—well—I'm counting on *Pretty
> Lady.* It's got to support ME for a long time to come.

He strides toward door, grabs the doorknob, and hesitates; when he turns around, his mood has changed. He
is now down to business.

BARRY (in almost a wail):
> But Julian—wait a minute—

Jones takes a step forward.

MARSH (all business now):
> Remember, my contract makes me Boss, with a cap-
> ital B—what I say goes. Make the chorus call for ten
> o'clock tomorrow! (He bows briskly, flips a curt
> half-salute, and exits.)

Jones and Barry stare glumly at each other, as though
neither knew exactly what to say. Then, shrugging,
Jones walks to his desk and sits down.

BARRY (shrugging as he walks to his own desk):
> If he isn't crazy, he's giving a first-rate imitation of a
> man who is!

JONES (concernedly):
> But suppose the guy should pass out on us?

BARRY (glumly):
Then New York would see its first TRIPLE funeral!

DISSOLVE TO

39. CLOSE-UP THEATER MANAGER IN BOX OFFICE
nodding as his listens to phone.

MANAGER:
Yeah—yeah—okay. (Hangs up, speaks over shoulder.) Say—Jones 'n' Barry're doing a show!

40. CLOSE-UP MAN AT DESK
CAMERA shows his back and head, and SHOOTS from behind him, and over his shoulder, revealing a sheet of paper in his hand. CAMERA is close enough, so that the top of the paper contains printing that is legible. It reads:
PRESS NOTICE:
The office of Jones and Barry today announced that "Pretty Lady," a musical
. . .
A desk sign, partially reversed reads:
DRAMATIC EDITOR
A phone stands before him on the desk, and he holds the receiver in his left hand, as he glances at the paper in his right.

DRAMATIC EDITOR (speaking softly):
This is straight, honey. The word just came in. Jones and Barry are doing a show!

41. CLOSE SHOT GIRL IN MAN'S ARMS
on couch as she answers phone.

GIRL (into phone):
Thanks—honeybunch—'bye! (Hangs up; to man.) Jones and Barry—doing a show!

Man rises unceremoniously, adjusts hair and tie.

MAN (starting out):
Maybe I work! See ya later!

42.   CLOSE SHOT   GIRL IN KIMONO AT WALL PHONE
in boarding house hallway.

GIRL (yawning):
Thanks—big boy—for the tip. (Hangs up.)

Crosses to stair banister, CAMERA PANNING with her.

GIRL (calling up stairwell):
Hey, darling! Jones an' Barry're doin' a show!

43.   LONG SHOT   UP STAIRWELL
as four men's heads appear leaning out over rails.

MEN (in quick succession; boisterously):
There IS a Santa Claus! Ok-ay, America! Coming!
Wait for Baby!

44.   EXT. MED. SHOT   MANHOLE IN STREET
with cover off and sign: Men at Work.

TRUCK UP TO:

45.   CLOSE SHOT   DOWN INTO MANHOLE
Two greasy telephone linemen working. One plugs
tester phone on line and listens.

FIRST LINEMAN (turning to partner):
Jones 'n' Barry're doin' a show.

SECOND LINEMAN (wearily, after aiming carefully and
spitting tobacco juice at blowtorch flame; diffidently):
I'll take a malted milk!

First lineman flashes central.

46.   CLOSE-UP   GIRL OPERATOR AT PHONE BOARD
Light flashes and she plugs in.

OPERATOR (singsong):
Bry-unt—offish—al!

47.   CLOSE-UP   FIRST LINEMAN

FIRST LINEMAN (in tester phone):
Testing . . . Jones 'n' Barry's doin' a show!

48. CLOSE-UP SWITCHBOARD OPERATOR

OPERATOR (as myriad lights flash on board):
You're telling me? Okay.

49. CLOSE-UP FLASH FEMININE LIPS CLOSE TO PHONE
LIPS:
Jones—

50. CLOSE-UP FLASH MAN'S EAR AT RECEIVER

FEMALE VOICE OFF:
and—

51. CLOSE-UP FLASH MAN'S EYES
bulging excitedly.

FEMALE VOICE OFF:
Barry—

52. MULTIPLE TRICK SHOT FOUR HEADS AND SHOULDERS

YOUNG MAN ABOUT TOWN:
Jones and Barry—doing a show!

CHORUS GIRL:
Jones and Barry—doing a *show!*

WHITE-HAIRED BUSINESSMAN:
Jones and Barry—*doing* a show!

MASCULINE DAME, VIOLETS IN HER LAPEL:
Jones and Barry—*doing* a *show!*

53. CLOSE-UP CLOCKFACE FILLING SCREEN
hands at eight o'clock. Hands make two complete revo-
lutions to ten o'clock. They move faster and faster as
they revolve, ticking of clock increasing in tempo with
their increase in speed.
    Superimposed on clockface at same time we see fol-
lowing quick wordless DISSOLVES.

1. MED. SHOT   BED AND STAND WITH ALARM CLOCK
Alarm rings. Feminine arm reaches from under covers,
revealing pretty sleepy girl, and grabs clock.

QUICK DISSOLVE TO:

2. CLOSE SHOT   EDGE OF BED, GIRL'S BARE KNEES
as she reaches down, lifts stocking and sock into scene,
tosses away sock, grabs other stocking, and draws
stockings up over shapely legs.

QUICK DISSOLVE TO:

3. FULL SHOT   GIRL'S FIGURE IN STEP-INS AND BRASSIERE
arms upstretched, wiggling into dress that hides head
and face.

QUICK DISSOLVE TO:

4. CLOSE-UP   COFFEE CUP
Slim, jeweled girl's hand, with elaborately manicured
and tinted fingernails, delicately dunks cruller.

QUICK DISSOLVE TO:

5. CLOSE-UP   VANITY CASE MIRROR
reflecting girl's bowed lips as little finger rubs on lip
rouge.

QUICK DISSOLVE TO:

6. CLOSE SHOT   TAXI STEP
Girl's foot and ankle, in spike-heel slipper and sheer
hose, steps down to curb.

QUICK DISSOLVE TO:

7. FULL SHOT   LOW ANGLE   STAGE DOOR STEPS
Parade of hurrying girls' feet up step to door.

SUPERIMPOSED SHOTS FADE OUT TO LEAVE:

54.   CLOSE-UP   CLOCKFACE FILLING SCREEN
hands at ten o'clock—customary Western Electric clock
buzz for hour sounds.

QUICK DISSOLVE TO:

55.   INT. FULL SHOT   BARE STAGE   42ND STREET THEATER
crowded with boy and girl candidates for ensemble.

Over babble of voices are heard rehearsal pianist picking out scraps of tunes at piano and assistant stage manager, MacElroy, shouting for order.

Andy Lee bustles in across stage.

56. MED. SHOT AT PIANO
As Andy enters, pianist looks up from keyboard.

PIANIST:
   H'ya, Andy?

ANDY (nodding greeting):
   Too good to be true! (MacElroy comes up and joins them.) How's the turnout, Mac?

MAC (shrugs):
   'Bout fifty-fifty. Half of 'em are dumb and the other half are dumber.

Andy turns to appraise crowd. Suddenly he catches sight of Lorraine and scowls.

57. CLOSE-UP LORRAINE
Smiling affectionately and waving coyly at Andy.

58. CLOSE-UP ANDY
reacting, discomforted and embarrassed.

JERRY'S VOICE OFF:
   Little Lorraine's been hitting the bottle again!

MAC'S VOICE OFF:
   Yeah—the peroxide bottle!

Andy tries to scowl forbiddingly.

59. MED. SHOT AT PIANO
Jerry winks wisely at Mac, who grins. Andy jerks his eyes from Lorraine.

ANDY (uncomfortably):
   Tell that dame I'm in conference—PERMANENTLY!

He hastens off scene. Jerry nudges Mac.

JERRY (with a snicker):
That gal sticks to him like dandruff to a blue suit!

MAC (chuckling):
Well, I could go for a dish of *that*, myself!

60. MED. SHOT   SIDE OF STAGE
as Andy hurries off, glancing angrily back over his shoulder.

LORRAINE'S VOICE OFF:
Hey—Andy—An-dy darling!

Andy stops peevishly. Lorraine joins him.

ANDY (exasperated; whispers out of the side of his mouth):
Listen, nitwit—will ya lay off that darling stuff . . .
Lay off . . . or do you want us both to be laid off?
Yuh wanna get me canned? (Looks around furtively.) You're in—you're set—now scram!

LORRAINE:
Dar-ling—you're just too sweet—the way you keep spoiling me!

Andy almost shudders as she pats his arm affectionately.

GIRL'S VOICE OFF:
I BEG your pahdon!

Andy turns jumpily.

ANDY:
It's okay. This is a two-way street!

61. CLOSE SHOT   ANN LOWELL
Peke under one arm, monocle in eye, posed nonchalantly, leaning on walking stick.[6]

ANN (very ritzy):
    Are you—by any chawnce—the—oh—what is that
    word—the stage manager?

62.   MED. SHOT   ANN, ANDY, AND LORRAINE
    Andy, taken aback and awed, just stares mouth agape.
    Lorraine recognizes Ann, smacking the vision boldly on
    shoulder.

LORRAINE:
    Why ANN! Come out from under that accent—I see
    you!

Ann's monocle tumbles from her eye, as she grabs Lorraine by both shoulders, grinning.

ANN:
    Lolly—DAR-ling!

LORRAINE (to Andy):
    You remember Ann Lowell?

ANDY:
    "Anytime Annie"? Say—who could forget her! She
    only said no once, and then she didn't hear the
    question!

LORRAINE (looking at the monocle):
    Y'been abroad?

ANDY (wisecracking):
    For years!

ANN (squelching Andy with a look):
    Not exactly . . . but my deah . . . I HAVE been
    moving in the veddy BEST circles!

ANDY (sneering):
    Yeah—but when you move in circles, you never get
    anywhere!

Lorraine slaps Andy on the shoulder, as much as to say:

"Isn't he the one, though," and Ann gives him a dirty look, as we hear:

MARSH'S VOICE OFF (peremptorily):
 ANDY! Where's Andy Lee?

Andy jumps guiltily, glares at the two girls for having detained him, and hastens in the direction of Marsh.

63.　MED. SHOT　AUDITORIUM FROM STAGE
 Marsh stands at orchestra pit rail. Man secretary hovers nearby. Several rows back of Marsh, Abner, Jones, and Barry are taking seats.

ANDY'S VOICE OFF:
 Right here—Mr. Marsh!

64.　FULL SHOT　APRON AND FRONT OF AUDITORIUM
 as Andy faces Marsh from footlights.

MARSH (all business):
 Line 'em up, Andy.

ANDY (turning away):
 Yes, sir. (To girls.) Come on, girls—

Marsh leans forward studying girls intently.

65.　FULL SHOT　STAGE　FROM MARSH'S ANGLE
 as Andy and Mac herd girls to places.

MAC (shouting):
 Quiet now—quiet!

ANDY (officiously):
 Show girls, right—mediums an' dancers, left!

The girls weave about, Mac and Andy scurrying among them.

66.　MED. SHOT　LORRAINE AND ANN AMONG CROWD
 Tough little chorine glimpses Ann's Peke, cane, and

monocle and laughs derisively. Ann freezes her with haughty stare turning to Lorraine.

ANN (ultra-English again):
Pleasant summah in Deauville, deah?

LORRAINE (taking cue, just as ritzy):
Chawming—but Sir Gawge is reahlly impossible at times!

CHORINE (jeers, nudging companion):
Get Minnie th' Mountaineer!

ANN (turning hotly, herself again):
It musta been tough on your mother—not having any children! [7]

As she speaks, someone bumps Ann from behind. Her monocle pops out of her eye, much to her disgust, and falls to floor. Lorraine looks down dismayed.

INSERT   CLOSE-UP   MONOCLE ON FLOOR
as girl's heel crushes it to pieces.

BACK TO SCENE:
Lorraine, concerned, looks commiseratingly at Ann. Ann, quite unruffled, opens purse.

INSERT   CLOSE-UP   OPEN PURSE
full of monocles as Ann's hand selects new one.

BACK TO SCENE:
as Ann with perfect poise screws new monocle in eye.
DISSOLVE TO or QUICK WIPE OFF TO:

67.   FULL SHOT   STAGE DOOR LOBBY
with corridor leading off to dressing rooms, and stairs leading up to dressing rooms and down to basement. Stage doorman reads newspaper at his little desk. Three hard-boiled girls are smoking and talking.
Street door opens and two workmen enter, carrying between them a huge property box. Their expressions indicate that it is plenty heavy. As CAMERA TRUCKS

closer, we see, under the box, a pair of beautiful legs, walking in step with the workmen. Suddenly the legs stop uncertainly and turn toward camera. The workmen continue off scene, revealing Peggy Sawyer looking timidly around.

The three hard-boiled girls look at her openmouthed, nod to one another in chorus, and one of them, winking to the others, steps forward.

FIRST GIRL:
Looking for somebody? Or just shopping around?

PEGGY (diffidently):
Could you tell me where I'll find the gentleman in charge?

FIRST GIRL (pertly; points down corridor):
Second door on your right!

Second girl starts to speak, stealthy kick from third girl stops her.

PEGGY (turning away down corridor):
Thank you.

Girls exchange amused winks and grin after her.

THIRD GIRL (calling after Peggy):
Don't knock—he's expecting you!

SECOND GIRL (protesting dumbly):
But that's—

FIRST GIRL (silencing her):
Sh-h-h!

68. MED. SHOT   PEGGY IN CORRIDOR
Pauses at door, looks up at sign which we see in CLOSE-UP. Sign reads:

MEN

She hesitates, turns back puzzled, and, shrugging, enters first unmarked door on her left.

69. CLOSE-UP PEGGY REVERSE ANGLE
stopping inside door, aghast at what she sees.

PEGGY:
OH!

70. FULL SHOT DRESSING ROOM FROM PEGGY'S ANGLE
A young man in B.V.D.'s is leaning over, back to her,
tying shoe. He straightens up and turns to face her.

MAN (surprised):
Sa-a-ay! What's the idea? (Reaches for robe.)

71. FULL SHOT DRESSING ROOM

PEGGY (stammers):
Oh—er, they said you—er—weren't you expecting
me?

BILLY (wrapping robe around him; puzzled):
No, but you'll do!

PEGGY:
Er—I—I don't understand!

BILLY:
That makes us even. I don't either.

PEGGY:
Oh, but—isn't this the—

BILLY (misunderstanding):
No, but I'll show you where it is.

PEGGY:
It isn't an "it", it's a "he"!

BILLY (nonplussed):
Say, maybe I'M wrong, but let's start this all over
again. I'm Billy Lawler, one of Broadway's better
juveniles.

PEGGY (disappointed):
> Oh—I thought you were—IMPORTANT. I mean I thought you were the dance director. I'm Peggy Sawyer.

BILLY (attracted and smiling innocently):
> That's the way a lot of people feel about—juveniles. Only most of 'em aren't so . . . frank! You're new to show business—aren't you?

PEGGY (haughtily):
> Oh—I've had experience!

BILLY (skeptically; as he looks at her with feigned sharpness):
> How—many—shows?

PEGGY (bluffing):
> Why any—number—of— (She weakens suddenly.) This'll be my—first—if they'll take me.

BILLY (warmly):
> Don't you worry, honey— (He pats her arm affectionately.) They'll take you—you can't miss. Say— I'll take you in myself! Come on. (He takes her by the arm.) I'll steer you right up to the big shot himself!

Looking at her with suddenly awakened interest, he guides her out of his dressing room and back down the corridor from which she's just come.

72. FULL SHOT   INSIDE STAGE DOOR
The three hard-boiled girls laugh loudly as Billy and Peggy approach.

FIRST GIRL (razzing):
> A short order of ham—COMING OUT!

BILLY (looking at three girls disparagingly):
> Not good—but loud! (To Peggy.) Take a good look

at 'em NOW—honey—'cause once they make that
BACK line, you'll never see 'em again.

FIRST GIRL (mockingly):
Well—if it isn't Little Lord Fauntelroy and the Village Maiden!

SECOND GIRL (laughing):
Made in New York—and all points west!

Ignoring the cracks, Billy, still guiding Peggy by the
arm, stops at the end of corridor and points down the
short, narrow corridor that meets it at right angles to a
portion of the bustling stage.

BILLY:
Right in there—the boss is Julian Marsh—a fellow
in a light grey felt.

MacElroy, bustling up the short corridor leading to the
stage, suddenly blocks her way.

MAC:
Where you headed, sister—chorus?

Peggy, startled, nods and looks hopefully to Billy. Billy
winks placatingly to Mac and nods. Mac raises his eyebrows and looks suspiciously from Billy to Peggy and
back to Billy again and shrugs.

BILLY:
She wants to see Marsh.

MAC (nodding toward stage and stepping aside to let
Peggy and Billy pass; turns to three girls):
That'll just about make Marsh's day perfect!

He continues off scene as CAMERA PANS from LONG SHOT
of Billy and Peggy walking on stage, to the three girls.

FIRST GIRL:
The chorus'll be her FIRST stop.

THIRD GIRL (sneering, and looking meaningly after Billy):
> And you don't have to be a mind reader to know her second!

73. FULL SHOT   STAGE AND FRONT OF ORCHESTRA
About sixty-five girls wait stage left for consideration. Downstage right and left and upstage are grouped two, 12, and 12 girls respectively, who have already been inspected and judged by Marsh, who is now inspecting another eight girls lined up across the apron, skirts raised high. Andy and Mac as before carry out his nodded instructions.

Marsh points to one of eight, jerking head stage right. Mac sends girl to join other two.

74. MED. SHOT   ANN AND LORRAINE
among nervous candidates, at side of stage. They cynically watch process of selection. Peggy moves in beside them, watching in big-eyed interest.

ANN (with yawn of disgust):
> Not a calf in a carload!

Peggy overhears and laughs spontaneously.

LORRAINE (noticing Peggy, grinning):
> First offense, kid?

Peggy nods, shivers ecstatically. Ann and Lorraine regard her with smiling sympathy.

PEGGY:
> Ye-s—but I don't think . . . maybe . . . I ought to tell 'em that.

LORRAINE (understandingly, but with sarcasm):
> OF COURSE not—and they'll NEVER guess!

PEGGY (wistfully):
> Do—you think I'll do?

LORRAINE (assuringly):
  I only know what I read in the papers—but you look all right to me!

MARSH'S VOICE OFF (crisply):
  Next eight!

Peggy jumps nervously. Ann takes her arm and propels her toward stage.

ANN:
  Stick with us, baby! And you'll come in on the tide!

The three make a break for the stage apron.

75. MED. SHOT MARSH IN FRONT ROW OF ORCHESTRA
as Andy, elaborately casual, joins him, with a disarming, innocent grin. Marsh gives him a quizzical look, then turns back to stage.

MARSH (to girls on stage):
  Turn slowly—let me see the legs, please.

76. MED. SHOT LINE OF GIRLS FROM MARSH'S ANGLE
PANNING along line with Marsh's glance, hesitating on Peggy, Ann, and finally Lorraine. All girls hold up their dresses above the knees.

77. CLOSE SHOT MARSH AND ANDY

ANDY (insinuatingly):
  Okay, those three on the right. If I were you, Mr. Marsh, I'd keep 'em!

Marsh looks understandingly at Andy, forestalls a smile, and then looks back at girls.

78. MED. SHOT PEGGY, ANN, AND LORRAINE
who are the three on the right.

79.   CLOSE SHOT   ANDY AND MARSH

MARSH (dryly):
> I suppose if *I* don't, YOU'LL have to! Lorraine
> again, huh? Andy, you're a panic! (Andy looks
> sheepish and remains silent. Marsh feigns gruff-
> ness.) All right, have it your way!

Andy's innocent dead pan bursts into a seraphic smile.

80.   FULL SHOT   FRONT OF STAGE AND ORCHESTRA
including Marsh, Andy, and row of girls with Mac.

MARSH (calling ironically):
> Oh, Mac— (indicating three, jerking head right)
> okay—by special request of the copyright owner!

81.   MED. SHOT   ANN, PEGGY, AND LORRAINE
among select few by proscenium arch. Lorraine winks
broadly at Ann and the smiling Peggy, then claps Ann
jovially on back. Ann's monocle leaps out of her eye and
splinters on floor. Peggy gasps in dismay. Ann gives
Peggy an unconcerned smile and digs again into her
purse.

INSERT   CLOSE-UP   PURSE OF MONOCLES
as hand selects new one.

BACK TO SCENE:

PEGGY (excitedly):
> Does that mean that we're selected?

LORRAINE (sagely):
> Uh-uh. Just held for future reference.

PEGGY (disappointedly):
> Oh . . .

ANN (wisely):
> But don't let THAT throw you. (Looking cynically
> at Lorraine.) LOLLY'S got connections!

LORRAINE (saucily):
   Yeah? And that ain't all that Lolly's got—either!

Peggy's jaw drops, and then she chuckles as Ann screws new monocle into eye.

WIPE OFF TO:

82.   CLOSE-UP   CLOCK FACE FILLING SCREEN
   as hands spin rapidly from eleven to two o'clock. Superimposed is multiple trick shot of myriad girls' legs, faces, feet, hands, etc., which DISSOLVE OUT leaving clock face in clear at two o'clock.

WIPE OFF TO:

83.   MED. SHOT
   Sixteen show girls standing on stage—they have been picked. Ann, Peggy, and Lorraine watching.

MARSH'S VOICE OFF:
   That make sixteen? Show girls?

MAC (to Marsh OFF):
   Yes, sir.

MARSH'S VOICE OFF:
   Get the names and addresses and let them go!

The sixteen selected show girls crowd around Mac, who gets out a pencil stub and paper.

MAC:
   Speak up, ladies.

FIRST SHOW GIRL (impressively):
   Diana Lorrimer—333 Park Avenue!

ANN (snorting, to Lorraine):
   And is HER homework tough!

WIPE OFF TO:

84.   FULL SHOT   STAGE
   Forty weary chorus girls wait around stage. Chorus boys disconsolately lounge about as they have all day.

Half a dozen handpicked girls cluster near the proscenium arch. Eight are lined up across apron, each in
turn being called on to do a brief, simple dance step.

Marsh, a fierce relentless driving machine, paces back
and forth in first row of orchestra. Jerry pounds at
piano.

Commotion as Dorothy Brock enters from stage door
accompanied by buzz of comment and sweeps across
stage to footlights. Andy signals Jerry to stop playing,
and activity stops momentarily.

DOROTHY (businesslike, to Marsh):
Julian—have you that revised script for me?

MARSH (beckons secretary):
Right here, Dorothy.

Secretary hands Marsh manuscript case as Abner lumbers down aisle into scene.

ABNER (smiling eagerly, his thumbs hooked into the
armpits of his waistcoat):
Hullo, Dor-othy. I've been waiting most all day, just
to see you. (He looks at her appraisingly and looks
around him.) Um—you sure do look—beautiful.

DOROTHY (slightly annoyed):
Hello, darling. I really did hurry—but I've just been
on the go—right since early morning—horrid old
show business—you know.

ABNER (starting to clamber onto the stage):
Well, in MY business, I always say . . .

MARSH (bluntly):
Your business is kiddie cars, isn't it? Well, I'll promise to stay out of kiddie cars if you'll promise to stay
out of show business. (He turns his back on the
nonplussed Abner and hands a script up to
Dorothy.) Here—let's get going with this. (He gives
Abner—off scene now—a dirty look.) Unless you
have some other plans!

85.   MED. SHOT   ANN, PEGGY, AND LORRAINE
They are sprawled wearily on the floor, in a group.

LORRAINE (to Peggy and Ann):
    He certainly isn't MY idea of a big moment!

PEGGY (innocently):
    Who?

LORRAINE (indicating Abner, off scene):
    The big butter-and-egg man!

PEGGY:
    You mean butter and eggs are his *business?*

LORRAINE (disgustedly; she shakes her head sadly as she
turns to look at Peggy):
    Say—you CAN'T be only eighteen; a girl just
    couldn't get that dumb—in only eighteen years.

ANN (maternally; to Peggy):
    No, honey—kiddie cars are his *business*.

PEGGY:
    But what's he doing here?

ANN:
    Here? Oh—this is his PLEASURE! He's the angel
    behind this show. With Dorothy's looks—and
    Marsh's brains—and HIS money— (She shrugs.)
    How can we miss!

PEGGY (getting it):
    Oh!

LORRAINE (peevishly looking at Dorothy):
    Some dames get all the breaks all right. (She turns
    to Ann, talking across Peggy.) I don't know how
    they do it. Just tell me ONE THING what that
    dame's got that *I* haven't—will ya?

ANN (nonchalantly):
    Sure. ABNER DILLON!

86.　MED. SHOT　DOROTHY, MARSH, AND ABNER

Dorothy is on stage; Marsh is in the pit; Abner sits un-comfortably on the stage, his legs dangling into the pit, uncertain as to what his next move ought to be.

ABNER (looking at Dorothy):
　　But—but we're goin' to dinner, ain't we?

DOROTHY:
　　Oh, you poor lamb—I WAS to have dinner with you tonight, wasn't I. But you will excuse me, won't you—I must dash RIGHT down to the dressmakers—for a fitting—you understand . . .

ABNER (puzzled as he rubs his chin):
　　Oh, er . . .

DOROTHY:
　　I knew you would. (She waves her script at Marsh as she starts off.) 'Bye, you old slave driver. (She blows a faint kiss to Abner.) Tomorrow night, dear. 'Bye!

87.　MED. SHOT　ANN, PEGGY, AND LORRAINE

Still resting as they watch Dorothy.

ANN (raising her eyebrows and looking maternally at Peggy):
　　. . . And the technical name for that, my darling, is the great American runaround!

88.　EXT. FULL SHOT　STAGE DOOR ALLEY

Dorothy's car waiting, stagehands lounging about. Dorothy comes from stage door and enters limousine. Chauffeur closes door after her, and car pulls away down alley. CAMERA TRUCKS with it to corner where it pauses.

　　Dorothy opens door, leans out, and beckons someone off scene.

89.   MED. SHOT   MAN IN DOORWAY

DOROTHY'S VOICE OFF (calling softly):
   Pat!

Pat Denning hurries toward car, CAMERA PANNING with
him. With elated smile, Dorothy draws him into
limousine. Door slams shut and car proceeds.

DISSOLVE TO:

90.   CLOSE SHOT   DOROTHY AND PAT IN TONNEAU OF CAR
As Pat settles himself, Dorothy, beaming, snuggles
close to him and sighs contentedly. As the car moves,
we see the street traffic through the car window back of
them.

DOROTHY:
   Waiting long, Pat?

PAT (thoughtfully):
   Long enough!

DOROTHY (pouting):
   Ooh—we *are* grouchy—aren't we?

PAT:
   Not grouchy—it isn't that— (He squirms uncomfortably, feeling in his pocket for a cigarette.)

DOROTHY (solicitously reaching for the automatic lighter
and holding it for him as he puffs):
   Then what is it?

PAT (grimacing):
   I don't know—it's just that I—well—this
   skulking—and hiding—and sneaking out of doorways and staying in the shadows— I guess—
   well—I'm beginning to feel like a criminal—always
   in hiding—always afraid to come out in the open.

DOROTHY (consolingly):
   But Pat darling—you mustn't— (She puts her finger
   to his lips and, leaning suddenly toward him, kisses

85

him tenderly.) There now . . . there's nothing
criminal in *that*—is there?

PAT (smiling hopelessly):
No . . . not in *that*.

DISSOLVE TO:

91.   FULL SHOT   FRONT OF STAGE AND MARSH IN ORCHESTRA
Eight girls, including Ann and Peggy, are lined across
apron trying to appear bright and chipper. End girl
finishes her simple dance step and waits hopefully.
Marsh waves hand to Andy, with sharp shake of head.
Piano stops.

MARSH (voice crackling):
Won't do! (Points to Ann.) You—same routine!

Piano starts again. Andy herds first girl away as Ann
throws herself vivaciously into dance routine. Marsh in-
terrupts her after three steps.

MARSH (sharply):
That's enough!

Music stops. Ann looks annoyed.

MARSH (grinning suddenly):
I remember—you worked for me before?

ANN (gushing English):
Indeed I did—and I *loved* it!

MARSH (sarcastically):
I was worrying about that—get over there!

Ann favors him with an elaborate smile and struts to
select group by proscenium.
Piano starts as Peggy steps nervously forward. She
misses a routine chorus step but Marsh notes her tempo
is perfect. Jerry stops automatically, leaving Peggy
stranded in middle of step, embarrassed.

MARSH (kindly):
Never mind.

PEGGY (smiles eagerly):
  I KNOW I can learn the steps, Mr. Marsh. I studied
  dancing five years!

MARSH (amused by her earnestness):
  Where?

PEGGY (embarrassed):
  Er—er—Sioux City.[8]

The chorus, lolling in the background, laugh loudly.

MARSH (smiling faintly):
  That's all right. (He nods toward the laughing
  chorus.) Most of these ladies have never even heard
  of Brooklyn—although they've been living there all
  their lives! (To people on stage, severely now.)
  QUIET—PLEASE!

ANDY'S VOICE OFF:
  Quiet please!

MAC'S VOICE OFF:
  Quiet—please!

MARSH (waving Peggy away):
  There are probably a lot of worse places than Sioux
  City. (He indicates the selected bunch, and as
  Peggy turns elatedly to join them, he beckons the
  next girl.)

92.   MED. SHOT   PEGGY IN GROUP OF GIRLS   TERRY STANDING
  NEAR HER

PEGGY (excitedly):
  Gee, does that mean I'm finally IN?

TERRY (butting in):
  Yeah—*in* for a long night's work! (He looks her over
  from head to toe, appraisingly.) And it'd be just MY
  luck to have him toss you out!

87

PEGGY (turning to Ann, uncertainly):
Did he say something? (She indicates Terry.)

ANN (dryly):
Not a word! (She gives Terry a dirty look.)

93.   CLOSE-UP   WRISTWATCH
marking four o'clock. Piano is pounding a tune, and feet
are tapping.

                                        DISSOLVE TO:

94.   CLOSE-UP   WRISTWATCH
marking 6:15. Piano stops.

                                        TRUCK BACK TO:

95.   CLOSE SHOT   MARSH
as he looks up from watch to stage.

MARSH (impatiently):
Well—what is it now?

96.   MED. SHOT   AT FOOTLIGHTS
Andy leaning over to speak to Marsh, with apprehen-
sive laugh.

ANDY (confused):
Guess we slipped up somewheres, chief. Looks like
we're one girl shy!

MARSH (sarcastically):
That's great. GREAT! All we need now is *one* girl,
and *one* dance director who can count up to forty
without a pad an' pencil. (He waxes hotter.) Well,
DO SOMETHING! *Get* another girl. You don't expect to stand there and shake a blonde out of your
pant leg do you!

BILLY (hurrying from orchestra seat to Marsh's side):
Mr. Marsh—I don't want to butt in . . .

MARSH (angrily):
A lot of people are like that—

88

ANDY (butting in; placatingly):
I—I'll have a girl here first thing in the morning!

MARSH (sarcastically):
That's just ducky. I can hardly wait!

BILLY (stubbornly):
Gee, Mr. Marsh—that's what I've been trying to tell you. You don't have to wait . . . (He points off scene.)

97.   MED. SHOT   PIANO FROM THEIR ANGLE
From behind it protrude a pair of trim female legs, the skirt pulled up revealingly.

BILLY'S VOICE OFF (eagerly):
. . . and she's a swell dancer too—I've been watching her all day! You picked her once but she got eliminated the third time through.

ANDY'S VOICE OFF (in delighted relief):
And mother used to tell me there was no Santa Claus!

98.   FULL SHOT   STAGE AND FRONT ROW OF ORCHESTRA

MARSH (calling):
Hey! You—behind that piano!

All pause expectantly. The legs do not move.

ANDY (bellowing):
HEY! You—you with th' legs!

Still no response. A chorus girl laughs.

MARSH:
Quiet—please!

MAC (irate):
Quiet—pul-leeze!

ANDY:
> Quiet—please! (Striding toward piano.) What's th'
> big idea—huh?

99.   CLOSE SHOT   PIANO WITH LEGS PROTRUDING
Andy enters, looks behind piano ready to bawl girl
out. His jaw drops in surprise and amazed amusement.

100.   CLOSE SHOT   GIRL BEHIND PIANO   FROM ANDY'S ANGLE
Peggy, dog-tired, sound asleep, head slumped against
piano, a blissful smile on her face.

ANDY'S VOICE OFF:
> We-ell—I'm a—!

101.   CLOSE SHOT   ANDY AND SLEEPING PEGGY

ANDY (grins, rousing her):
> Hey—kid!

Peggy starts up, frightened.

PEGGY:
> OH!

ANDY:
> Come on, the boss wants a look at ya again.

Andy pulls Peggy out where Marsh can see her.

102.   FULL SHOT   STAGE AND GROUP IN ORCHESTRA
Rubbing eyes, little-girl fashion, Peggy stumbles forward with rueful, disarming smile at Marsh.

MARSH (with a laugh):
> Why—it's little Miss Sioux City. (To Andy.) She'll
> do. (Turning away.) They're all yours, Andy!

Marsh clears his throat and climbs upon a chair.

MARSH:
> *All right*—now—you people. Everybody quiet! And
> listen to me! (He pauses for a moment as the people

on the stage surge toward him and quietly regard
him.) Tomorrow morning—we're going to start a
show. We're going to rehearse for six weeks and
then . . .

DISSOLVE TO:

103. CLOSE-UP ANN IN THE GROUP
She is mugging fearfully as she painstakingly attempts
to get her monocle finally adjusted while—

MARSH'S VOICE OFF (continuing):
We're going to open on schedule time—

CAMERA PANS BACK TO SCENE same as 102.

MARSH (continuing):
. . . and I *mean* schedule time. You're going to
work and sweat and work some more—you're
going to work days . . .

DISSOLVE TO:

104. CLOSE-UP LORRAINE
She is frantically trying to blow a fly off her nose without success, as—

MARSH'S VOICE OFF:
. . . and you're going to work nights—and you're
going to work between times . . .

CAMERA PANS BACK TO SCENE same as 102.

MARSH:
. . . when I think you need it—you're going to
dance until your feet fall off—and you aren't able to
stand up . . .

DISSOLVE TO:

105. CLOSE-UP PEGGY
as she listens, open-mouthed, excitedly and attentively.
CAMERA PANS slowly to Ann, who, in a final facial
paroxysm, drops her monocle and mouths the word
"Damn!"

MARSH'S VOICE OFF:
   . . . but six weeks from now—we're going to have a SHOW! Now some of you . . .

CAMERA PANS BACK TO SCENE same as 102.

MARSH:
   . . . have been with me before and you know it's going to be a tough grind! (He looks slowly around the assembled group.) It's going to be the toughest six weeks you ever lived through. Do you all get that? Now anybody who doesn't think he's going to like it had better quit right now! (He looks around the circle inquiringly, but there isn't a single dissenting voice.) Nobody? (He nods with satisfaction.) Good! Then that's settled! We start tomorrow.

He climbs down off his chair and, waving a curt "good night," walks determinedly off scene.

ANDY (shouting as the circle breaks up):
   That's all—kids. Lyrics—first thing in the morning!

MAC:
   Lyrics in the morning—kids.

The company breaks up chattering as the various members make wearily for the exits.

                           DISSOLVE TO:

106.   FULL SHOT STAGE SET FOR NUMBER FILLING SCREEN framed by proscenium arch. Completely decorated but empty of people. Off scene, man whistles tune from *Pretty Lady*.
   Suddenly two mammoth hands enter scene from above.

                    TRUCK BACK QUICKLY TO:

107.   FULL SHOT MINIATURE STAGE ON TABLE
Marsh, in lounging robe, arranging miniature drapes, whistling as he works.

Stops whistling and raises head, listening.

DISTANT VOICE OFF (calling insistently):
Julian! Yoo-hoo! Oh, Marsh!!!

Marsh shrugs impatiently and turns away from table.

108. FULL SHOT   LIVING ROOM   MARSH'S APARTMENT
Marsh crosses to window and looks out.

109. EXT. FULL SHOT   DOWN AT SIDEWALK FROM MARSH'S
ANGLE
through open window, which is 'on second floor.
Jones, looking up at window, sees Marsh and waves
arms urgently.

JONES (calling up to Marsh):
I gotta talk t'you, Julian! Lemme in!

110. FULL SHOT   LIVING ROOM
Marsh nods.

MARSH (calling down):
All right—come on up.

Marsh crosses and presses buzzer, releasing latch on
downstairs door. He crosses to table, twitches miniature
stage curtains shut, and turns off its lights. Takes cigar
from table and lights it.
Jones enters breathless and excited.

JONES (looking for place to lay his hat. He nods absently
as Marsh takes it from him):
I thought I'd better come over and tell you, Julian
. . . It looks like we're in trouble . . .

MARSH (placidly):
The word has a familiar sound.

JONES:
But this is serious. You know, of course, Abner
Dillon is putting up the dough for this show . . .

MARSH (bored):
I knew he wasn't hanging around because you liked his face.

JONES:
Well, er—HIS interest in the show is Dorothy Brock.

MARSH (nodding calmly):
Even I was able to gather THAT.

JONES:
Well, we stand a first-rate chance of having him withdraw his financial support right *now* . . . DID YOU GATHER THAT?

MARSH (frowning with concern now):
But why?

JONES:
Because dear little Miss Brock is two-timing him right under his very nose—that's why!

MARSH (grimacing):
Who with?

JONES:
A fellow—he used to be her partner—for years—when she was in vaudeville. Now she's come up in the business and he just hangs around—he was out of town somewhere, and he just got back last week. If Dillon finds it out—and if he doesn't he's dumber than I thought even HE could be—he'll just walk out. We'll be sunk. That's what! If we don't do something quick . . .

MARSH (thoughtfully):
Tried applying a little dough to the problem? Give the Romeo a hundred bucks and ship him off. Get him out of the way.

JONES (shaking his head):
> You don't know this guy Denning—Pat Denning,
> that's his name! He's not the kind of a guy that—
> gets sent places—just like that.

MARSH (rising and crossing thoughtfully to his desk
where he consults a small notebook):
> I see—hard-boiled—huh? Well . . . (He picks up
> the telephone and starts dialing.) It's going to be
> just too bad—but— (His face hardens.) No vaude-
> ville chump is going to ruin MY show!

JONES (apprehensively):
> What—what are you going to do?

111.   CLOSE SHOT   AT DESK
Jones watches Marsh suspiciously.

MARSH (waiting for his number to answer):
> I'm going to talk it over with Murphy—a *friend* of
> mine from downtown—*he* never DID like vaude-
> ville.

JONES (approaching Marsh nervously):
> Slim Murphy?[9] You can't! Listen—I don't wanta get
> mixed up with Murphy or any other gangsters—

MARSH (smiling calmly):
> No? Well—what's one man's meat is another man's
> Murphy. (Fiercely now.) I told you what this show
> meant to me—well—THIS IS WHAT IT DOES
> MEAN TO ME! (He talks into phone now.)
> Hello—Murphy? This is Julian Marsh. I'm okay,
> thanks. Yep. Murphy—you've got to do me a
> favor— Did you ever hear of Dorothy Brock? (He
> smiles.) Good! That makes it so much easier.
> Well—here's the idea— It seems there's a certain
> guy by the name—
>   CUT TO:

112.   MED. SHOT   SLIM MURPHY AT PHONE IN POOL PARLOR

He talks into wall telephone, turning his head fre-
quently to watch the progress of a game of pocket
billiards going on behind him. A group of roughnecks
stands around the pool table on which one man is shooting and, as Murphy pauses, we hear the click of the balls
and the guttural exclamations of the onlookers.

Murphy leans on elbow against wall and talks into
phone. He wears a vest over a collarless shirt, with
prominent sleeve bands, and as he talks, he laboriously,
absently prints out the beginning of the word Denning
on the wall beside the phone.

MURPHY:

I getcha—Mister Marsh—sure— (He turns around
angrily on the group behind him and calls to them.)
Hey—you mugs! What do ya think I'm wearin'—
EAR phones? (And turns back to the telephone.)
It's as good as done—an' say—y'ain't gonna forget
me on ducats fer th' new show—are yuh? (He
smiles broadly.) O-kay!

FADE OUT

FADE IN

113.   MED. SHOT   PAT AND DOROTHY ON AN OUT-OF-THE-WAY
PARK BENCH

They sit close together on a bench beside Central Park
Lake. We see them in the faint illumination of a park
lamppost. Both stare thoughtfully into the mirrorlike
lake. The far-off lights twinkle in the apartments across
the park. Dorothy's hand suddenly moves toward Pat's.
He raises his to see what she's placed in it.

PAT:

Looks like money—feels like money—it IS money.
(He shakes his head slowly as he crumples up the
bills and finds her hand.) Not another nickel—
honey. I—it just can't be done anymore—that's all.

DOROTHY:

Why, Pat. Don't be silly. We've always shared—and shared alike—haven't we? What's come over you?

PAT:

Getting a sudden attack of manhood—possibly—or maybe—things are different now.[10]

DOROTHY:

You mean because of—because they're *starring* me now?

PAT:

Let's quit kidding ourselves, Dot. You're headed for big things— Me—I'm getting to be a regular anchor around your neck. This business of only seeing you when nobody else is looking, of keeping hid in doorways and always under cover, has got me down. (He smiles.) Besides . . . I've been getting myself some education. I've discovered that they have a name for a man who doesn't work . . . and accepts money—from a woman. It isn't a very nice name, Dot.

DOROTHY:

But I owe everything I am to you, Pat. It was you—and that little act of ours—that started me in all this . . . You trained me and coached me and taught me all I know . . . I haven't forgotten . . .

PAT (smiling and trying to change the subject):
The act?

DOROTHY:

I haven't forgotten—THAT—either. It was grand, Pat—but really grand—wasn't it?

PAT:

Sentimentalist! Or maybe your memory's gone back on you. It was terrible.

DOROTHY:

You didn't think so—then!

PAT:

You mean I didn't SAY so—then. (He turns half facing her.) Don't you see? You've gone ahead—YOU rated it. I've stayed behind, where I belong, I guess.

DOROTHY:

You've deliberately *kept* yourself behind, Pat.

PAT:

They wanted you, honey. They never wanted me. (He shakes his head a little sadly, but he is anything but bitter.) Do you know—I'm beginning to think it's a good thing we didn't marry, Dot.

DOROTHY:

And THAT was *your* fault too! *You* broke it off.

PAT:

If I had as much courage—now—as I had then—I'd break it off entirely NOW, Dot. I'd never see you again. It would be better for us both.

DOROTHY:

Please, Pat! You're talking like a child. (She suddenly clings to his arm. He rises, fussed, and braces up.)

PAT:

Come on, young lady. Getting late—it's time I got you home.

They rise slowly, Dot clinging to his arm.

DOROTHY:

Oh, Pat—I wish you wouldn't feel like you do!

PAT:

I wish I wouldn't too . . . but I do!

FADE OUT

FADE IN

114. INT. CLOSE-UP   MUSIC CUE SHEET ON PIANO RACK
corrected in pencil, scrawled across top of page: "It
Must Be June—Pretty Lady—Act I."

JERRY'S VOICE OFF (lugubriously):
Better run that chorus again, Andy.

TRUCK BACK TO:

115. MED. SHOT   AT PIANO

ANDY (wearily):
All right—you kids—we'll try it once again—but in
English this time.

Andy nods to Jerry, who strikes chord.

PAN TO:

116. FULL SHOT   ENSEMBLE
in motley rehearsal clothes, grouped about holding papers with typed lyrics, as they start to sing as Jerry
plays.

VOICES (singing):
When lovers spoon beneath the moon
And learn to croon a dreamy tune—

117. CLOSE-UP   JERRY
hunched over keyboard, eyes half-closed, cigarette
drooping from lip, mechanically pounding out tune.

VOICES OFF (singing):
When roses red begin to bloom
It must be June, it must be June—

118. MED. SHOT   ENSEMBLE
PANNING around circle of bored faces.

VOICES (singing):
When you are true to someone who
Is true to you then skies are blue
If you love me as I love you—

119. CLOSE-UP PEGGY AND LORRAINE
Peggy intently earnest as Lorraine, dead pan and bored, opens mouth, ceases singing, and yawns widely.

VOICES OFF (singing):
    It must—it must be June,
    Not September or November,
    April, August, or December—

120. CLOSE-UP ANN
Prattling in singsong.

VOICES OFF (singing):
    It must, it must, it must, it must,
    It must, it must, it must, it must,
    It must be June.[11]

As last note dies, Ann raises eyes to heaven.

ANN (in childish treble):
    An' God bless Papa an' Mama!

121. FULL SHOT ANDY AND ENSEMBLE REVERSE ANGLE
as Ann's line gets laugh.

ANDY (with biting sarcasm):
    Great! Ya beat Jerry t' th' finish by two lengths!
    (Claps hands.) Come on—positions! We gotta get
    them routines down.

ANN (caustically):
    A lyric may be down—but it's never out!

Ensemble scatters as stagehands move chairs away.

122. FULL SHOT STAGE
Ensemble in positions for number as Jerry plays intro-duction.

ANDY (on apron, loudly):
    Now, you babies—GIVE!

Ensemble starts dancing, some counting, others reciting
words they remember.

WIPE OFF TO:

123. FULL SHOT   LOUNGE AT BACK OF AUDITORIUM
Marsh rehearsing entire cast of principals. Piano and
Andy's scolding voice heard occasionally in distance.
Abner sits watching as Dorothy and leading man are
finishing a scene.

DOROTHY (script in hand, without feeling):
"Things can never be the same now—" and so and
so and so—down to "breakfast in bed."

MARSH (to leading man):
That's where you take her hand, John.

The leading man does so. He and Dorothy look ques-
tioningly at Marsh, who consults script.

MARSH:
The scene ends with you two on the steps—then we
go right into the duet. Get it? (Dorothy and leading
man nod.) Number's over! Let's pick it up—page
forty-two.

DOROTHY (coming forward, crossly):
Julian—that next scene sounds as though it was put
together by the stage carpenter!

AUTHOR (springs up aggressively from seat):
Huh?

DOROTHY (ignoring author):
It's completely out of character—makes me common!

AUTHOR (angrily):
But that's the twist, Mr. Marsh. This is *one* musical
with a plot. Change this scene—and you might as
well *throw away* the book!

MARSH (dryly):
> Maybe you don't think *that's* an idea!

AUTHOR (wildly):
> But—but—!

MARSH (waving him away):
> Never mind. (To Dorothy.) I'll go over the scene again at lunch, Dorothy. Take it as it stands for now.

Mollified, Dorothy starts back to her place, with venomous look at irate author.

DOROTHY (spitefully):
> Someday—somebody with *brains* will write a show—for authors!

AUTHOR:
> And what a job it'll be to find somebody with brains to act in it!

LEADING MAN (seriously to Marsh):
> Julian—that first speech of mine. Is it moody—you know, with a bit of pathos? Or is it courageous— fiery—with a—a—lift?

MARSH (nodding, just as serious):
> Yes and no—but don't quote me!

Leading man glowers peevishly.

MARSH (patiently):
> Can we run through it now, please?

Overalled boss electrician ambles in from backstage.

ELECTRICIAN:
> Mr. Marsh—fer that foist act *finally*—ya want full ambers in th' foots—and red in yer front border?

MARSH (succinctly):
> No. Listen, Mike—I told you! At end of chorus— dim out the blues—bring up your floods—then give

'em all you got with borders and foots on full—ALL amber—no reds.

MIKE (grinning amicably):
    Gotcha, boss. That's all I wanted t' know. (Exits.)

Marsh turns back to principals in their places.

MARSH:
    All right now—let's try it! With a little *feeling! Punch!* And I don't mean the kind that comes in bowls!

    WIPE OFF TO:

124.   CLOSE SHOT   ANDY AT FOOTLIGHTS
    watching dance number. Piano beating out different tune now. Andy's whole body alive, feet tapping out routines. He is driving dancers hard.

125.   FULL SHOT   CHORUS   FROM BACK OF STAGE
    Andy in background suddenly claps hands savagely.

ANDY (exasperated):
    Hold it! Hold it! (He glares at three girls on end.) What are you trying to do—finish, win, place, and show?

Piano stops, girls pause drooping.

ANDY (shaking head):
    All right—you can take a couple o' deep breaths. I gotta talk t' Marsh—but DON'T go away.

Andy clambers across orchestra pit on board bridge and starts up aisle toward front of house as chorus drifts wearily to sides of stage.

126.   MED. SHOT   BILLY BY BENCH AT SIDE OF STAGE
    as Peggy enters and drops wearily down on bench. She smiles companionably at Billy, who grins in friendly sympathy.

BILLY (encouragingly):
    You're doing fine, kid—for a beginner!

PEGGY (gratefully):
> Thanks. I'm trying. Say, I was so scared I walked around the block four times before I had courage enough to even come and apply for a job.

BILLY:
> It's plenty tough—all right—but you'll get along.

PEGGY (nods ruefully):
> I wouldn't mind—if I could only get that routine set.

Terry barges in with hostile look at Billy.

TERRY (to Peggy, kindly, condescendingly):
> Lissen, sister—I'll show you them taps. (Taking her arm authoritatively.) Come on over here!

PEGGY (getting to her feet):
> Taps? Say—I can do a tap dance on my ear. What bothers *me* is that routine!

TERRY (with supreme confidence):
> Then I'm just what the doctor ordered— Come along!

Terry leads her off without a glance back at Billy.

127.   MED. SHOT   PIANO IN CORNER
Jerry gets up for stretch as Peggy and Terry enter. Terry starts slow version of routine as Peggy watches intently. Jerry regards them with despair.

TERRY (the teacher):
> Now, look—

JERRY (groans):
> You kids're gluttons for punishment!

PEGGY (smiling):
> Mr.—Mr.—this boy's showing me—

TERRY (explaining):
    I'm just trying to make her—

JERRY (grumbling, turns away):
    Trying to *make* her, is right!

Jerry exits morosely as Peggy goes on with lesson.

128.   MED. SHOT AT APRON OF STAGE
    Marsh and Andy coming over bridge meet Jerry.

    ANDY:
        What are they doing—warming up?

    JERRY (thumbing toward piano, sardonically):
        He is! (He smiles.) That always kills *me!* Just a couple
        of hoofers breakin' their fool necks, thinkin' they'll
        be stars some day.

    Marsh and Andy follow Jerry's look off scene.

129.   CLOSE SHOT TERRY AND PEGGY
    side by side now, hoofing away at routine.
                          PAN DOWN TO:

130.   CLOSE-UP PEGGY'S AND TERRY'S FEET
    dancing together in tempo.

131.   MED. SHOT MARSH AND ANDY AT APRON
    Marsh turns smiling from watching Peggy and Terry.

    MARSH (to Andy):
        Let's look at the number. We haven't got all day!

    ANDY (calling to ensemble):
        All right, everybody! Dancers—up here! We'll run
        through "It Must Be June" again! Jerry! Ready?

    MAC (echoing):
        Ready, Jerry?

    JERRY'S VOICE OFF (gloomily):
        O-kay!

132.   FULL SHOT   STAGE

Ensemble take former positions. Jerry starts playing chorus and ensemble starts singing and dancing.

VOICES (singing):
> When lovers spoon beneath the moon
> And learn to croon a dreamy tune—
> When roses red begin to bloom
> It must be June, it must be June;
> When you are true to someone who
> Is true to you then skies are blue
> If you love me as I love you,
> It must—it must be June,
> Not September or November,
> April, August, or December,
> It must, it must, it must, it must,
> It must, it must, it must, it must,
> It must be June.

"IT MUST BE JUNE" © 1933 WARNER BROS. INC. Copyright Renewed. All Rights Reserved. Used by Permission.

133.   MED. SHOT   MARSH AND ANDY AT APRON

VOICES OFF (singing):
> When you are true to someone who
> Is true to you then skies are blue—

MARSH (breaking in, with sweeping gesture):
> It's *out!*

ANDY (shouting off):
> Hold 'er, Jerry!

Piano stops; ensemble stops and stands waiting.

MARSH (making a face as though he smelled something):
> That'll be about enough of that. It smells!

Conroy, the composer, jumps onto the stage.

CONROY (incredulously):
Y' mean you don't like this number?

MARSH (sarcastically):
Sure I like it. I've liked it since 1905. Like it . . . ?
What do you think we're putting on . . . a revival?
It's out—the whole number—see?

CONROY (in feigned amazement):
Why, Mr. Marsh—that number'll be a RIOT!

MARSH (bitingly):
That's exactly what *I'm* afraid of. (He looks at his
wristwatch and turns to Andy.) Dismiss, Andy
. . . Hour for lunch.

Marsh, ignoring Conroy, turns away, leaving him dis-
gruntled and speechless.

134. FULL SHOT STAGE
as Andy shouts to company.

ANDY (bellowing):
Dismissed, everybody! One hour f'r lunch!

MAC (echoing):
Dismissed, everybody! An hour f'r lunch.

ANDY:
Be back at one-thirty—or ELSE!

Company makes a break for exits with jabber of small
talk.

135. MED. SHOT INSIDE STAGE DOOR
Terry enters and stands waiting. Shakes head several
times as chorus boys leaving pantomime invitations to
eat. They get it, and wink understandingly. Terry
shoves hands in pockets, jingles coins, pulls them out,
and looks down at them in palm of hand.

INSERT CLOSE-UP COINS IN TERRY'S HAND
A quarter, three dimes, two nickels, and a penny.
BACK TO SCENE:
Terry frowns, shakes head dubiously, then shrugs, dismissing it unconcernedly. As he stuffs coins back in pocket, Peggy hurries by. Terry stops her.

TERRY:
> Gonna eat?

PEGGY:
> Why—sure.

TERRY:
> How about throwing yourself in front of a steak . . . with me?

PEGGY:
> Why I—I—sure—I guess it'll be all right!

She takes his arm and they start briskly off scene.

DISSOLVE TO:

136.   INT. MED. SHOT   CORNER OF "YE EAT SHOPPE" RESTAURANT (FORTY-SECOND STREET AND EIGHTH AVENUE)
Peggy and Terry occupy a table in one corner. At a table, by himself, opposite, sits Billy, interestedly reading a copy of *Variety*. At a table directly in front of Terry and Peggy sit Ann and Lorraine.

TERRY:
> Sure . . . some day the big shots are gonna get wise to me, and then watch little Terry go!

LORRAINE (audibly):
> Yeah—right—out—the—window!

PEGGY:
> Well, I hope I'll be right along with you, Terry.

TERRY (misunderstanding):
> You could do worse!

PEGGY (confused):
Oh—I, er—didn't mean . . .

TERRY:
Say . . . you don't have t' be delicate with me!

ANN (audibly; to Lorraine):
Y'know—I hate that mug, and someday I'll think of a reason.

LORRAINE (just as audibly):
I don't NEED any reason.

TERRY (looking at Ann and Lorraine, at their table, and burning, as he addresses Peggy, for their benefit):
Say—teamin' up wouldn't be such a sour idea. Besides . . . (he looks pointedly at Ann and Lorraine) it'd get you out of this—show girl en-viron-ment . . .

ANN (sneering):
Humph! Environment! He got THAT word out of the lyrics, all right!

PEGGY (suddenly noticing Billy, who is eyeing the scene disapprovingly, smiles, and turns to Terry):
Well, that's awfully nice . . .

TERRY (magnanimously):
Think nothin' of it, kid. Why say—you stick around an' in no time at all you'll be almost as good as me . . .

WAITRESS (noisily slaps down two orders of beans):
BEANS!

DISSOLVE TO:

137.   CLOSE SHOT DAILY PAD CALENDAR
shooting down to it. Superimposed dancing feet in series of multiple dissolves kick off pages—July 28 to August 5—time lapse ten days.

WASH OUT TO:

138.   CLOSE-UP   MARSH
barking angrily at dancers off scene as piano strums a
number to accompaniment of slapping feet.

MARSH (relentlessly):
Watch that tempo—watch it! Get those feet off the
floor! Get into it now! Faster—faster! (Claps hands
sharply.) Stop! Stop! That's BRUTAL.

Piano stops.

139.   FULL SHOT   STAGE
as chorus stops dancing, panting but fresh. Marsh
stands facing them, unruffled. Andy stands useless, but
attentive, nearby.

MARSH (with vast sarcasm):
May I remind you that *Pretty Lady*'s out-of-town
opening is not far away! It has been advertised as a
musical comedy with dancing. If it's not asking too
much—will you please show me some? (Harshly to
pianist.) Once again, Jerry!

Piano starts again. Chorus doggedly attacks number
once more. Marsh glances at wristwatch.

INSERT   CLOSE-UP   WRISTWATCH   (SOUND OF PIANO)
marking 10:15. Piano tune blends into music of different
show number as we

DISSOLVE TO:

INSERT   CLOSE-UP   LADY'S WRISTWATCH   (SOUND OF
PIANO)
diamonds and platinum, marking 2:30.

140.   CLOSE SHOT   DOROTHY
as she looks impatiently at her wristwatch, then off
scene wrathfully.

141.   FULL SHOT   STAGE
Marsh driving chorus, who look fagged out. Marsh rips
off coat and tosses it to Andy, who passes it to Marsh's

secretary. Dorothy moves from near proscenium arch to Marsh, center of apron.

142.   MED. SHOT   DOROTHY AND MARSH

DOROTHY:
> If you're *never* going to rehearse me in the second act, I'd like to go home.

MARSH (without taking eyes from chorus or losing a beat):
> I'll get to you! Wait! (Sharply to dancer.) You—in the green—last row—jump into it! Now look alive, will ya?

Dorothy shrugs, furious, and stalks away. The dance goes on.

143.   CLOSE SHOT   ABNER AND JONES
seated in orchestra. Abner, drowsy from heavy lunch, dozes. Jones nudges him. Abner's eyes blink open.

JONES (meaningly):
> Havin' fun?

ABNER (wearily surfeited):
> After three weeks of this, a leg ain't nothin' t' me but somethin' to walk with. (He grimaces wearily.) Otherwise, I'm okay.

JONES (dryly):
> Did you say "O.K."—or "A.K."?

144.   FULL SHOT   STAGE
as number ends. Marsh turns to join Dorothy. Andy takes command, his first sign of activity.

ANDY (very efficient):
> All right, kids—rest!

MAC (repeating):
> Okay, kids—rest!

145. MED. SHOT   PEGGY
in chair near wall. Terry comes over.

TERRY (cheerily):
How's it going, baby?

PEGGY (weakly):
Still alive . . . I think. (Brightening.) I finally got
that routine, thanks to you.

TERRY (ultra-Broadway):
Forget it. Say, when I get time I'll show you
routines that Marsh or Andy never even thought of!

146. MED. SHOT   GIRLS INCLUDING ANN AND LORRAINE
as they droop panting on bench or lean against wall.
Ann, without ceremony, sits wearily on floor, tenderly
feeling her feet. Lorraine sinks down beside her. They
look off scene toward Peggy and Terry.

LORRAINE (watching Terry):
That guy is certainly a ham on the make!

ANN (shaking her head):
Nope! You can CURE a ham!

LORRAINE (looking fagged):
After a morning like this, I'm not worrying about
anybody else. Just think o' my condition . . . I'm
ANEMIC!

ANN (raising her eyebrows):
Well, why don't you make the rat marry you?

147. CLOSE SHOT   GIRL
leaning against piece of scenery, eyes closed. Falling
asleep she lurches, almost loses her balance, catches
herself, props open her eyes, and yawns.

148. MED. SHOT   TWO GIRLS AND MAN
lying on roll of canvas, dead to world.

DISSOLVE TO:

149. MED. SHOT MARSH AND DOROTHY
Behind them, you see Jerry at the piano. Marsh, his coat off, his shirt sleeves rolled up and his soft-collared shirt open at the neck. He is not freshly shaven and begins to show the strain of his work. As he waves his hand, Jerry strikes up a few bars of Dorothy's number, and as Marsh nods, Dorothy goes into her song.[12]

150. CLOSE-UP OLD-FASHIONED WATCH
with hunting case front, as pudgy man's hands open lid. Watch shows 6:10. Sound of chorus of duet number off.

151. CLOSE-UP ABNER
shaking head sleepily as he looks at watch.

152. FULL SHOT STAGE
Chorus hardly able to stand is going through duet number. Marsh now has tie off, collar is open, and hair is disarranged.

153. CLOSE SHOT PEGGY AND TERRY
dancing side by side. Peggy is all in, staggers. Terry notices this and eyes her apprehensively as he dances.

TERRY (between breaths):
Ya—all right—kid?

PEGGY (gritting teeth, forcing bleak smile):
I—I guess—so!

Peggy stumbles and goes out like a light. Terry jumps to catch her, carries her off stage assisted by Lorraine. PAN with them through lines of dancers. Billy hurries up.

MARSH'S VOICE OFF (brutal, commanding):
Places! Everybody! This is a rehearsal, not a rest cure—Mac! Take that girl outside!

Mac joins group at edge of stage. Reluctantly and with backward worried glances, Lorraine and Terry get back into the routine as Billy and Mac cart Peggy toward stage door.

154. EXT. FULL SHOT   STAGE DOOR IN ALLEY   DUSK
Pat stands waiting near stage door, lighting fresh cigarette from butt of old one as Peggy is carried out stage door by Mac and Billy. Stage doorman puts chair by wall, and they sit Peggy down.

MAC (hurrying Billy back inside):
Come on, Lawler, inside! The girl's okay.

Billy and Mac reenter stage door. An old actor at stage door, getting a breath of air, approaches Peggy and stage doorman. He shakes his head disapprovingly, as he looks from Peggy to Pat.

OLD ACTOR:
They just about kill these youngsters . . . (he shrugs) and for what?

Peggy opens her eyes dizzily.

PAT (cynically):
For thirty-five a week—when you get it!

PEGGY (overhearing Pat; she speaks weakly and tries to rise):
Oh—I—I guess I—fainted!

The old actor moves back inside and Pat nods after him.

PAT:
Good guess!

PEGGY (wobbles to her feet):
I—I guess I'm all right now. (She stumbles dizzily.)

PAT (grabbing her):
Bad guess. Now let ME play! (He takes her arm and sits her down again.)

PEGGY (smiling):
And what would YOU suggest, doctor?

PAT:
A little fresh air—and conversation.

PEGGY (looks concernedly inside):
But—Mr. Marsh . . .

PAT (consolingly):
Never mind Marsh. Let's sit this dance out!

PEGGY:
And if I lose my job?

PAT (smiling):
There probably just won't be any show!

PEGGY (smiling):
Umm—anyway—it's a nice IDEA!

PAT (archly):
You know—I have a *lot* of nice ideas. But I need ears
to spill them in.

PEGGY (flirtatiously):
Well—won't MINE do?

PAT (with feigned earnestness):
Very—VERY—nicely! (Quickly following up the
thought.) And when are your ears available?

PEGGY (kiddingly):
Oh—at all sorts of odd hours— You *must* look them
up sometime!

PAT:
Say— (approvingly) remind me to tell you I think
you're swell—will you?

PEGGY (smiling; as she rises, steady now; to Pat):
Thanks, doctor. Your prescription was great! Now
for the workshop!

PAT (smiling broadly):
Oh—but it has to be taken daily—to really do any
good!

PEGGY (she looks steadily at him):
> But it'll have to be ABSENT treatment, I'm afraid—!
> At least for the time being!

Peggy slips into theater. Pat realizes with dismay he never even learned her name. He lights another cigarette gloomily and paces up and down, waiting. Dorothy comes out stage door and starts toward her car. Pat steps forward. As Dorothy gets into car, stage door opens again and Abner comes puffing out. Pat turns his back and stands unobserved close to wall. Abner gets into car with Dorothy. The car rolls luxuriously away.

155.   CLOSE-UP   PAT
as he stares glumly after receding car.

156.   CLOSE-UP   DOROTHY
as she looks back at Pat, through rear window of receding car. She blows him a kiss.

157.   MED. SHOT   STAGE DOOR   PAT IN FOREGROUND, FROWN ON HIS BROW
as Peggy, Lorraine, Ann, and the numerous other girls drag listlessly out of the theater. Pat sees Peggy, smiles, and steps to her side.

ANN (yawning, as she goes on her way):
> One more day of this, and it's back to the laundry for little Annie.

LORRAINE:
> Well, anyway, that'd be a clean life! Ha! Ha! Ha!

PEGGY (catching sight of Pat for the first time and lagging behind):
> Why, doctor! You must—like it here!

PAT (smiling):
> I'm beginning to—but you see—I'm really not the doctor anymore. You are. I've become the patient. I thought I'd wait and get a little—advice.

PEGGY (getting the spirit):
Very well—but you might tell the doctor your name.

PAT (in mock seriousness):
Oh—I can't do THAT! But my initials are Pat Denning! (He breaks into a broad grin.) Er—what would you advise for a man who is both hungry and lonesome—and who simply HATES to eat alone?

PEGGY (getting it):
Company!

PAT:
Excellent! Er—did *you* have anyone in mind—in particular?

PEGGY (shaking her head):
Did *you?*

PAT (nods, earnestly, with a boyish, sincere grin):
Will you?

PEGGY (nods slowly in acceptance, grinning disarmingly also):
I'm very much afraid—I will!

LAP DISSOLVE TO:

158.   MED. SHOT   ATOP FIFTH AVENUE BUS
Half a dozen couples occupy as many seats and are necking, oblivious of everything around them. Peggy and Pat occupy a rear seat.

159.   CLOSE SHOT   PEGGY AND PAT
As CAMERA TRUCKS back to them, bus goes over a bump and we see them both joggled ludicrously.

PAT (putting his arm on the seat back, behind Peggy):
Ugh! The royal road to romance!

PEGGY (sighing contentedly):
After ten hours of rehearsing this is heaven!

PAT:

How'd you ever come to do it—this chorus job—I mean? Win a bathing beauty contest?

PEGGY (smiling and burlesquing it):

Nope—just the will to succeed! You've read about THAT!

PAT (somewhat bitterly):

Somewhere—a long time ago.

PEGGY (sympathetically):

You aren't very happy—are you, Pat?

PAT (thoughtfully):

Happy? I remember that word—from my crossword puzzle days.

PEGGY (looking squarely at him):

Tell me—what's got you down?

CONDUCTOR (as his head and shoulders appear at the top of the bus stairwell):

Forty-second Street!

They both laugh and turn for a fleeting glimpse of the conductor as he disappears again down the stairwell.

PEGGY (seriously):

But you haven't told me yet . . .

PAT:

What's got me down? (He shrugs.) It's a—long story . . .

PEGGY:

I've lots of time!

PAT (smiling ruefully):

Well—once upon a time . . . isn't that the way ALL stories should begin? (He looks at her for confirmation.) A man had a girl of whom he was very, very fond. They worked together and played together—but—well—they didn't advance together. You see? The girl became a great success . . . and the man— (Peggy looks at him curiously) remained a—flop—but success didn't go to the girl's head—she still loves—the man . . . and because the man's a flop—he doesn't know just what to do. Tell me—my newfound playmate—what would *you* advise?

PEGGY (soberly):
I'd—advise a brand new deal. I'd—start all over from the beginning. Do you know—I believe that if I was in love—like the man—I wouldn't let anything in the whole wide world stand in my way!

PAT (thoughtfully):
So that's the way it's going to be—with you!

PEGGY (with assurance):
And that's the way it *ought* to be with . . . (she looks directly into his eyes) with HIM!

160.   EXT. MED. SHOT   NIGHT
ENTRANCE PEGGY'S BOARDING HOUSE (ON FORTY-SECOND STREET BETWEEN EIGHTH AND NINTH AVENUES)

Peggy says good night to Pat at door.

PEGGY (extending hand):
Thanks, Pat. It's been a wonderful evening.

PAT (holding hand a second too long):
Shall I see you again?

PEGGY:
I hope so, Pat! (They stall—sort of embarrassed. She turns to door.) Good night!

Pat turns away down steps. Peggy looks after him, then turns to door, digging in purse for key.

161. FULL SHOT SIDEWALK IN FRONT OF HOUSE
as Pat reaches sidewalk, two hefty men step up to him
from closed car at curb.

162. CLOSE SHOT PAT AND TWO MEN ON SIDEWALK
as heftier of two comes up close.

THUG:
> Ain't got a light on you, have you?

PAT (approaching and feeling in his pockets):
> Sure!

THUG:
> Don't happen to know a guy named Pat Denning,
> do you?

PAT:
> Why of course . . . I . . .

THUG:
> Never mind. We got a message for him. This Den-
> ning is a wise mug, but not wise enough. If he don't
> lay off this Dorothy Brock dame—it's gonna be just
> too bad . . . for DENNING! Get it?

PAT (taken aback):
> Er, all right—I'll—I'll tell him!

THUG (as he suddenly and brutally smashes Pat in the
face):
> Yeah? Well—THAT'S so you don't forget!

Pat falls to the sidewalk as first thug hops into waiting
car. Second thug starts for car, hesitates, kicks Pat hard
in the body, and then joins his companion in the car.

163. FULL SHOT SIDEWALK AND STOOP
Peggy turns in open door, sees second thug kick Pat
viciously. Their car leaps away as she rushes down to
him.

PEGGY:
Pat! Pat!

164.   MED. SHOT   PAT ON PAVEMENT
struggling up as Peggy enters to help him. Pat's face is
bruised and bleeding. He is groggy.

PEGGY (arms around him):
Who were they, Pat!?

PAT (suffering; shakes head in attempt at levity):
Friends! With good advice!

DISSOLVE TO:

165.   INT. FULL SHOT   PEGGY'S ROOM
Pat is lying upon Peggy's bed. Peggy, a glass in her
hand, sits at the foot of the bed beside him. Pat's coat is
off and his necktie is awry, and now and then he ruefully feels his chin.

PEGGY (curiously):
But Pat—if you and Dorothy Brock were
partners . . .

PAT (facetiously as he attempts a shrug):
I guess they're just keeping Dorothy safe now—
from bad influences—like me.

PEGGY:
But—but I thought that this—this Mr. Abner Dillon
was Dorothy's boyfriend!

PAT:
Evidently they don't seem to think so! (He rubs his
chin ruefully.) You see it's Abner Dillon's personal
interest in Dorothy that's responsible for his *financial* interest in the show. It looks like they figure me
as the well-known monkey wrench—

As Peggy hands him the glass of liquid which she has
been holding, a strapping landlady appears through the
open door. The landlady, taking in the spectacle quickly
frowns in frank suspicion.

LANDLADY (sourly):
> What kind of a house do you thing this is? You get that drunk outta here right now!

Pat looks toward her, startled. Peggy, equally startled, rises.

PEGGY (in dismay):
> But Mrs. Holt . . .

166.   CLOSE SHOT   LANDLADY IN DOORWAY
with door across hall clearly visible behind her. As land-lady berates Peggy, this door opens quietly and a di-sheveled man, coat over arm, shoes in hand, stealthily slips out of room, as sexy girl, in blowsy kimono and clearly nothing much else, pantomimes him to caution and quiet. Door closes silently as man disappears.

LANDLADY (interrupting):
> *But* nothing. I got eyes. Just because there's a de-pression on—some folks think a landlady's got to stand for anything.

PAT (rising):
> But you don't know . . .

LANDLADY:
> After keepin' a roomin' house for nine years—there's nothin' I don't know! Now out he goes . . . and no more talk!

PEGGY (burning):
> Then if HE goes . . . *I* go too!

LANDLADY (turning on her heel and exiting):
> I'll probably be able to bear up under THAT blow, too!

DISSOLVE TO:

167.   EXT. MED. SHOT   NIGHT
SIDEWALK IN FRONT OF BOARDING HOUSE
Peggy, carrying hatbox, and Pat, with two bulging suit-

cases on ground beside him, stand at foot of steps. His face is definitely marked up.

PEGGY (smiling timidly):
  Well—where do we go from here?

PAT:
  Hotel?

PEGGY:
  I suppose so. But it'll have to be an inexpensive one. I've only got about a dollar and a half!

PAT (he frowns slightly as he digs his hand into his money pocket, his expression becoming more worried as he slowly withdraws his hand):
  How about . . . my place . . . ?

PEGGY (understandingly):
  Broke?

PAT:
  Not exactly—but not exactly flush, either.

PEGGY (wonderingly):
  Then it's your place—or a park bench, I guess. (She shrugs as Pat starts hopefully.) Well—let's try YOUR place . . . FIRST!

DISSOLVE TO:

168.   INT. FULL SHOT   PAT'S LIVING ROOM
in the Gothic Arms, corresponding to southerly of two end apartment buildings in Tudor City, foot of East Forty-second Street.

Peggy, slightly nervous, surveys room as Pat puts suitcases in corner. He deposits her hat, coat, gloves, and purse on table as Peggy crosses to tall window, looking down on lights of Forty-second Street stretching away toward Hudson River.

Pat, at table, mixes highball, picks up cigarette from box, and crosses to Peggy. Peggy, fascinated by view, does not turn.

169. CLOSE SHOT   PEGGY AND PAT BY WINDOW
Pat holds glass and cigarette.

PAT:
> Drink? (Peggy shakes her head.) Smoke? (Peggy
> shakes her head again.) Are you alive?

Peggy starts to shake head a third time, then realizes
what he said, and turns to him with puzzled half smile.

PEGGY:
> Barely . . . why?

PAT:
> Well, I mean . . . no drink, no smoke. Mind if I do?

PEGGY:
> Of course not.

Peggy turns back to gaze out of window. Pat tosses
cigarette toward table, sips drink, watching Peggy, then
drops his arm with careful carelessness about her
shoulder, and looks out of window with her.
  For a moment she does not notice, then feels arm's
pressure. She turns and looks at him dubiously, slips
unobtrusively from within his arm and moves out of
scene.

PAT (superficially contrite):
> My error!

Pat follows Peggy out of scene.

170. MED. SHOT   PEGGY NEAR TABLE
with a level look at Pat as he enters scene.

PEGGY:
> That's all right, Pat. I don't want to be wrapped in
> cellophane all my life . . . only . . .

PAT (understandingly, leading her to divan):
> Tired?

PEGGY (nestling down on divan):
Um-hum.

PAT:
TOO tired?

PEGGY (smiling mischievously):
Um-HUM!

PAT:
That sounds like a song!

PEGGY (stifling a yawn):
It is—an exit march!

But the couch is inviting and she drops onto it with a sigh of comfort—all in.[13]

PAT:
You don't have to hurry away.

Peggy gives him a suspicious little smile and leans back luxuriously, closing her eyes. Pat gets pillow from armchair, CAMERA PANNING with him. His normal inclination to go for this girl and his sense of fair play are at war. He returns and stands, pillow in hand, looking down at Peggy.

171.   CLOSE-UP   PEGGY ON COUCH FROM PAT'S ANGLE
Head back, eyes closed, chin and mouth uptilted invitingly. Her lips are parted in a blissful smile of complete relaxation.

172.   CLOSE SHOT   PEGGY AND PAT
as Pat leans down toward her, about to place pillow behind her. His face is close to hers, there is nothing to prevent his taking her in his arms and kissing her, but he hesitates. This suddenly hits him as much too easy. With quick revulsion of feeling he straightens up frowning and turns away.

173. MED. SHOT   PEGGY ON COUCH AND PAT
as he turns back on her.

PAT (almost harshly, back to her):
On second thought— (he chucks pillow viciously
back at chair) I guess you'd better go to bed!

Pat starts to light cigarette with nervous fingers. Peggy
opens her eyes, surprised, rises, moves around, and
studies the grim-faced Pat.

PEGGY:
All right—Pat. (She turns toward bedroom door.)

174. FULL SHOT   LIVING ROOM
as Peggy moves quietly to door and opens it. She stops
and turns. Pat stands as before, studying tip of cigarette.

PEGGY (in a small voice):
Good night.

Pat rouses and crosses to corner for luggage.

PAT (striving to be casual):
You're forgetting your luggage.

He carries suitcases to her at open door.

PAT:
Good night, youngster.

Taking suitcases, Peggy goes in, closing door after her.
Pat stands watching closed door.

175. MED. SHOT   INSIDE BEDROOM AT DOOR
as Peggy straightens up from putting bags on floor. She
looks at door, hesitates a moment, then reaches out and
turns latch, locking door.[14]

176. FULL SHOT   LIVING ROOM
Pat crosses, picks up his glass, turning back to look at
bedroom door. As he does, he glimpses his reflection in
mirror and chuckles.

177. CLOSE SHOT   PAT AND REFLECTION
as he raises glass, toasting his reflection, and drains his drink.

PAT (humorously):
You're not such a bad guy, after all.

Pat crosses to kitchenette alcove, CAMERA PANNING with him. He fills empty glass with water at sink, removes gardenia from buttonhole, places flower in glass, and puts glass in refrigerator. CAMERA PANS with Pat as he crosses to armchair, picks up pillow with wry smile, crosses to couch, arranges pillows, feels couch springs, and starts to remove coat and tie.

FADE OUT

FADE IN
178. CLOSE-UP   CARD TABLE
set for two: doilies, silverware, etc. Orange juice and toast at each place, electric coffee pot perking. Pat's hand comes into scene and lays gardenia at one place. Hand hovers over table, straightens doily, moves glass inch to right, silverware fraction to left.

TRUCK BACK TO:

179. FULL SHOT   LIVING ROOM
Table in foreground, closed bedroom door in background, as Pat arranges table, back to bedroom door. He steps back surveying his handiwork, cocking head to one side, as door opens behind him and Peggy emerges, fully dressed, blinking sleepily.

180. CLOSE-UP   PEGGY AT DOOR
as she sees Pat's activity and smiles brightly.

PEGGY (sniffing rapturously):
Mmmmmmmmmm—breakfast!

181. CLOSE-UP   PAT

PAT:
Optimist!

182.   FULL SHOT   LIVING ROOM
as Peggy crosses hurriedly to table. Pat holds chair and
Peggy sits.

PAT (pouring coffee):
   Happy landing!

183.   MED. SHOT   TABLE
Pat sits opposite Peggy, who eats and drinks.

PEGGY (looking happily around, as she munches a piece
of toast):
   This IS nice!

PAT:
   Like it?

PEGGY:
   I could sit like this all morning!

Suddenly her expression changes to one of dismay, and
she grabs his arm apprehensively and looks at his
wristwatch.

PAT (gently places his hand over hers, which rests on his
arm, and smiles):
   It's nine-forty!

PEGGY (in alarm):
   Nine-forty! (In a wail.) Oh, gee! I'll NEVER make it!

184.   FULL SHOT   LIVING ROOM
Peggy, toast in hand, with other hand grabs hat, purse,
and gloves from table, makes for door, which Pat opens
for her.

185.   CLOSE SHOT   PAT AND PEGGY AT DOOR

PEGGY (gesturing with piece of toast):
   Oh—my luggage! May I leave it here?

PAT:
   Unless you'd call THAT too compromising!

PEGGY (starting toward door):
    'Fraid I'll have to take that chance.

With a quick wave of her hand, she starts through door, hesitates, and turns around to look at Pat.

PEGGY:
    Pat—you really ARE a darling!

186.   FULL SHOT HALLWAY
    as Peggy hurries from Pat's apartment toward elevators. An overdressed but unshaven actor type pauses and watches her with a gleam of amused and approving understanding. Then, chuckling, he advances to door Peggy just left, coming face to face with Pat.

PAT (slightly disconcerted):
    Oh— Hello, Waring! [15]

187.   MED. SHOT INSIDE LIVING ROOM DOOR
    as Pat ushers Waring in and closes door.

WARING (with suggestive nod towards hall):
    Not bad!

PAT (gruffly):
    Wrong again!

Waring turns to lay aside his hat and stick and notes table for two. He looks at Pat, with a smirk, eyebrows raised. Pat ignores his look, and says nothing.

188.   FULL SHOT LIVING ROOM
    as Waring starts toward bedroom.

PAT (quickly):
    Coffee?

WARING (at bedroom door):
    No time. Just thought I'd look in—

PAT:
    What's the rush?

WARING (impressively):
I have an appointment.

PAT (interested):
Job?

WARING (nods):
Right. Stock in Philadelphia!

PAT (thoughtfully):
Philadelphia. (Hopefully.) Say—do you suppose there's a spot for me?

WARING:
Sure. Briskin told me to feel you out—they need a heavy—who makes good little girls go wrong. (He smiles and looks meaningly at the table set for two.) You're practically letter-perfect now. But what's the big idea?

PAT (ignoring his thrust):
No big idea. Dorothy and I are washing up. That's all. I'm getting out.

WARING (smiling):
So you finally got tired of being *Mister* Brock, under cover?

PAT:
Exactly. Tell Briskin I'm all set. What time do you leave?

WARING:
Eleven o'clock.

PAT:
Then I'll stop by for you at half past ten!

As Waring exits, Pat rises thoughtfully. Starts to open drawers to start packing.

189.   FULL SHOT   LIVING ROOM
as buzzer sounds, Pat straightens shoulders and goes to door.

190. MED. SHOT AT DOOR

as Pat opens door, revealing a ravishing Dorothy.

DOROTHY (pertly):
Hello, honey.

PAT (evenly):
Oh, Dot! Come in!

Dorothy crosses toward couch, CAMERA PANNING with her.

DOROTHY:
Let me look at you—

She sits on couch, apparently uneasy. Pat enters scene and stands offering cigarette. She pats place beside her on couch.

PAT (reservedly):
Same old Pat.

DOROTHY (looking at him sharply, as though trying to read his thoughts):
I wonder.

PAT (suspiciously):
Haven't gone serious on me again, have you?

DOROTHY (suddenly noticing Peggy's bags, and slightly put out and hurt; she ignores his question):
You . . . leaving town?

Pat looks startled. His eyes rove around the room and, with a relieved look, suddenly come to rest on something off scene.

191. CLOSE SHOT PEGGY'S BAGS IN BEDROOM DOORWAY

PAT'S VOICE OFF (hesitantly):
Er . . . yes . . . Philadelphia . . . stock job.

CAMERA PANS BACK TO:

192.   MED. SHOT   DOROTHY ON DIVAN, PAT STANDING NEAR

DOROTHY (hurt):
> Oh, Pat. Without TELLING me?

PAT (uncomfortably):
> It seemed best that way.

DOROTHY (quietly):
> Maybe . . . you're right. (Pat looks at her sud-
> denly, in surprise. She pats the divan cushion be-
> side her and continues.) Sit down, dear, I want to
> talk to you.

With a questioning glance, Pat walks slowly toward her
and sits down beside her.

DOROTHY:
> I've done a LOT of thinking too, since the other
> night. (Pat nods and lights a cigarette.) Pat . . . do
> you know what's wrong with me? Or rather with
> US? (Pat shrugs.) We've grown too necessary to
> one another. You've been content to rest in the
> shadows and see ME bask in the spotlight . . .
> simply because it's held us together. (He takes her
> hand in a friendly gesture.) My success has been
> YOUR failure.

PAT (interrupting quietly):
> My FAILURE, as you put it, has been my happi-
> ness.

DOROTHY:
> But Pat . . . you're capable of splendid things
> yourself. You're not a quitter. I've only wanted to
> help you . . . but I've been hurting you instead. I
> realize it now. That's why I came this morning! Pat
> . . . we're not going to see each other again for a
> long while. No more doorways, no more secret
> meetings. You're going out on your own, and make
> a success!

PAT (rising quietly and walking moodily toward window):
> I've made up my mind, too, but somehow, I can't *imagine* living without you, Dot.

DOROTHY (rising also, and looking off scene after him):
> Nor I without you. But it's *got* to be! It's GOT to be!

CAMERA PANS from Dorothy to Pat, who turns from window to look at her.

PAT (shrugging wearily):
> You're right, Dot, it's GOT to be—and maybe, someday . . . sometime . . .

DOROTHY'S VOICE OFF (as Pat turns back to look glumly out of window):
> Good-bye, Pat . . .

He doesn't turn around. We hear the door slam.

FADE OUT

FADE IN

193.　CLOSE SHOT　DAILY PAD CALENDAR
Shooting down on it. Superimposed dancing feet kick off pages—August 6—August 20—time lapse of two weeks.[16]

WASH OUT TO:

194.　MANHATTAN SKYLINE　　　　　　　　DAWN
Impressionistic shot.

DISSOLVE TO:

195.　CLOSE SHOT　MARSH
He is working under a terrific nervous strain. He is thinner, drawn, and beats a wild rhythm with his arms. He is in his shirt, collar open at the throat, and half open down the front. Beads of sweat stand out on his forehead, and there is the inevitable dead cigarette between his fingers.

MARSH:
> NO! NO! NO! STOP. Cut it, Jerry!

Wearily, he wipes the perspiration off his face, with a handkerchief that is already soaked. Jerry, at the piano, stops playing.

196.   FULL SHOT   STAGE
We hear Marsh, continue off.

MARSH'S VOICE OFF (bitingly sarcastic):
> Ladies and gentlemen, permit me to congratulate you. You are without a doubt the greatest, the most stupendous, the *lousiest* gang of hoofers ever assembled on one stage. Where's your tempo? Where's your rhythm? Where're your brains? (The last three questions work up to a fast, roarlike crescendo.) Now it's up to you. Not one of you leaves this stage tonight until I get what I want. (He speaks toward piano again.) Okay, Jerry!

Piano playing resumes, off scene.

DISSOLVE TO:

197.   CLOSE SHOT   ANDY
as he passes Ann in line.

ANN:
> Hello—Bluebeard!

ANDY (whispers):
> H'ya—kid!

ANN (flippantly):
> Oh—just a little touch of scarlet fever.

ANDY (just as flippantly as he moves along):
> That's fine—maybe it'll develop into something serious!

DISSOLVE TO:

198.   CLOSE SHOT   BILLY
wilted as he dances past a bedraggled Peggy.

BILLY (to Peggy, under breath, disgustedly):
What do you do when you got two left feet like mine?

PEGGY (breathless but consoling):
Just pick 'em up and lay 'em down!

DISSOLVE TO:

199.   CLOSE SHOT   MARSH BY FOOTLIGHTS
hair tousled, sweat-soaked shirt, open at throat, un-shaven, gaunt and sunken eyed, lighting one fresh cigarette after another from old one with trembling fingers and without a break, as he rages. He claps hands sharply.

MARSH (roaring angrily again):
Hold it! Jerry! Hold it! (Piano stops.) Some day, Lawler, some director's going to jail you for taking money under false pretenses. YOU'RE supposed to be a dancer. All you need is a couple of license plates and you'd look like a T Model Ford!

Marsh pauses to light fresh cigarette. Andy sidles up to him trying to be tactful.[17]

ANDY (persuasively):
Chief—they been goin' all night. It's four o'clock—

MARSH (viciously, loudly):
What of it!

ANDY (jerking thumb toward auditorium):
Brock's still waitin'!

MARSH:
So am I! I'll keep them at it 'til they get it—if it takes a week! Get out! (Andy fades away.) Take the last ten measures! Ready! (Claps hands.)

Piano off starts again. Marsh, watching Billy, frowns, shakes head, and starts off furiously toward Billy.

200.   MED. SHOT   FULL STAGE
CAMERA PANS slowly along line of dancing chorus and

comes to rest on one dumb-looking girl, who is hoofing heavily, with her mouth wide open.

201. CLOSE SHOT MARSH AND ANDY
watching dumb-looking girl.

MARSH (turning to Andy):
I bet I'm the first guy that ever kept HER up till four in the morning.

202. CLOSE SHOT TERRY AND ANOTHER CHORUS MAN
watching from side of stage.

TERRY (an envious sneer):
Get a load o' the *juvenile!* I didn't know we had *elephants* in the show!

Other chorus man looks at him and laughs.

203. FULL SHOT STAGE
as chorus makes exit and piano stops. Marsh and panting Billy are center stage; the chorus girls drop wearily as they reach sidelines.

MARSH (disgusted, to Billy):
Got it now?

BILLY (weakly nods):
I'm all in, Mr. Marsh, can I—

Marsh turns back, disregarding Billy's words, and waves to saturnine Jerry at piano.

MARSH (to Jerry):
Mr. Lawler thinks he'd better sing! So do *I!*

Jerry starts vamp. Billy checks a hot rejoinder on his lips, grits his teeth, and starts chorus of number. Ignoring him, Marsh walks toward footlights, starting new cigarette.

204.   CLOSE-UP   BILLY
wearily but bravely attacking song.

205.   CLOSE SHOT   PEGGY
as she lies back in chair panting. Terry enters, looks at
her and off at Billy, whose voice is heard over scene.

TERRY (jealously):
I never saw a juvenile yet ya didn't hafta lead!

PEGGY (defending Billy):
If it hadn't been for Billy Lawler, I wouldn't've *got*
this job.

TERRY:
An' if it hadn't of been for me—ya wouldn't of *kept*
it!
DISSOLVE TO:

206.   FULL SHOT   STAGE
as Marsh, ragged, unkempt, nervous, a dead cigarette
clenched between his teeth, runs shaky hands through
his hair and finishes scene rehearsal of Brock, Lawler,
and leading man. Around sides of stage are scattered
drooping members of ensemble.

MARSH (brutally):
What is this, amateur night? Have we been rehearsing for five weeks, or did I dream it? The show's
ragged. The number's ragged . . . May I remind all
you shining lights that THIS is the show that opens
tomorrow night? I AM in the right theater, am I
not? THIS IS the *Pretty Lady* company, isn't it? (Blis-
teringly.) The ALL—STAR—SHOW that's opening
. . . in Philadelphia tomorrow night?

Murmurs of surprise from everybody, as a number re-
echo "Philadelphia."

207.   CLOSE-UP   DOROTHY
reacting in startled dismay.

137

DOROTHY (to Marsh):
You mean Atlantic City, Julian.

208. CLOSE-UP PEGGY
as she darts a worried glance at Dorothy.

MARSH'S VOICE OFF:
I mean *Philadelphia!*

209. CLOSE SHOT MARSH
completing announcement.

MARSH:
Train leaves Penn Station at 1 P.M. *today*. Full dress
rehearsal Arch Street theater at seven o'clock.

210. CLOSE SHOT ANN AND LORRAINE

LORRAINE (unenthusiastically):
Philly-delphia—P.A.

ANN (peevishly):
And on Sunday it's P.U. (Pee-yew.)

211. MED. SHOT MARSH
putting on coat as Dorothy approaches nervously.

DOROTHY:
Julian—I don't want to go to Philadelphia—

MARSH (gruffly):
Who does?

DOROTHY:
But—I can't—for certain reasons—

MARSH (casually lighting cigarette):
When you become stage director we'll open in your
apartment—if you say so—but *now* it's Philadelphia! (He walks away.)

FADE OUT

FADE IN

212.   MED. SHOT   SPEEDING TRAIN WHEELS
We hear the clatter of train wheels, the roar of an engine whistle, the laughter and raucous conversation of people.

DISSOLVE TO:

213.   CLOSE-UP   BACKGAMMON BOARD
with pieces arranged as in middle of game. Noise of train off.

DISSOLVE TO:

214.   CLOSE SHOT   TWO MEN
Burly, unshaven, stagehands, engrossed in their game. Noise of train off.

DISSOLVE TO:

215.   MED. SHOT   TRAIN WHEELS
rolling slowly to a stop. Sound of puffing engine, tolling bell, and conductor's voice off as wheels jerk to a stop.

CONDUCTOR'S VOICE OFF:
Broad Street Sta-shun—Phil-adel-phee-ya.

216.   EXT. SHOT   PHILADELPHIA THEATER
Workmen are slowly arranging light bulbs in the final Y of *Pretty Lady*.

LAP DISSOLVE:

217.   CLOSE-UP   ORCHESTRA LEADER
in orchestra pit, raises baton. He is stripped to his undershirt, face beaded with sweat, voice hoarse, eyes glassy with weariness.

ORCHESTRA LEADER (a rasping croak):
Once more, boys. It's pretty tricky. Remember—four in a bar and a hold over that E in the final measure. Ready!

He raps baton on stand. Orchestra starts to play.

LAP DISSOLVE TO:

218.   FULL SHOT   AUDITORIUM
Shooting down over heads of company, ranged along
apron, toward first row of orchestra where Marsh
stands, backed by Barry, Jones, and company manager.

MARSH (coolly):
> Attention, please! We're going to run straight
> through the show tonight without stopping. Stay
> backstage—watch your cues—and keep quiet.
> Thank you. (Nodding to orchestra leader.) Over-
> ture! (Shouting off.) Drop the curtain!

219.   MED. SHOT   PEGGY
as she passes close to Billy on her way to line.

BILLY (hurriedly; in a half-whisper):
> Getting a kick out of it?

PEGGY:
> Of course—aren't you?

BILLY (slightly discouraged):
> I . . . don't . . . know. Do you suppose anybody'll
> even know I'm IN the show?

PEGGY (frankly):
> *I* will!

BILLY (looking furtively around):
> Does it really make any difference to you?

PEGGY (warmly):
> Gee—Billy . . . (she puts her hand on his arm
> lightly) I've always been for you! Ever since that
> first day!

As Billy slowly reaches to take Peggy's hand, we hear

ANDY'S VOICE OFF:
> Places now—everybody . . . Curtain!

220.   FULL SHOT OF STAGE FROM GRID
shooting down at an angle as curtain descends. Over-

ture plays off. Chorus scatters and arranges itself for opening number. Stagehands hurry to finish last minute jobs. Mac runs about placing girls and calling for missing ones. Suddenly at cue chorus is galvanized into life and starts to sing and dance as curtain rises and foot and spotlights hit faces of ensemble.

DISSOLVE TO:

221.   MED. SHOT   MARSH
hunched in second row, sharp eyes on stage as a number finishes. He springs to feet, advances to orchestra pit rail.

222.   CLOSE-UP   TWO PAIRS OF FEET PASSING AND REPASSING OVER NEW CARPET
CAMERA TRUCKS SLOWLY BACK to show MEDIUM SHOT of Jones and Barry, each wrapped in his own gloomy thoughts, parading up and down the aisle in opposite directions.

223.   MED. SHOT UP AT STAGE   MARSH IN FOREGROUND
as aged trouper veteran, dressed as old-time cab driver, enters to foots for patter scene.

MARSH (aggressively):
    The show's dying on its feet! Get in there and snap it up!

With brief nod in Marsh's direction, old man gathers himself together for a supreme effort.

CAMERA TRUCKS FORWARD to CLOSE SHOT of old man.[18]

OLD MAN:
    Forty-second Street! Sidewalks crowded with the ghosts of yesterday. Why—there's Eddie Foy stopping to shake hands with his old pal Raymond Hitchcock. Good old Sam Bernard. David Warfield—rest his soul. (Quoting.) "If you don't vant her—I vant her." And the grandest singer of

them all—Nora Bayes. I can hear her singing now
"Shine on Harvest Moon"—and the master of them
all—David Belasco. I remember them well and
they're gone—all gone—except me. (He pitches
forward and falls to the stage.)

224.   CLOSE SHOT   OLD MAN
His body twitches convulsively and is still.

225.   FULL SHOT   STAGE
as actor hurriedly bends over old man. Andy, Mac, and
company cluster around excitedly, and an excited jabber
rises.

226.   MED. SHOT   GROUP ABOUT OLD MAN
Marsh pushes way through, kneels by old man, feeling
heart, whispers to Mac, and rises. With gesture, Mac
calls couple of stagehands, and, with chorus man helping, they carry old man's body off into wings and toward stage exit. Marsh claps hands, Andy close beside
him, and calls loudly for company's benefit.

MARSH:
    Excitement—little too much for him. Nothing to
    worry about! He said before he fainted he hoped
    you'd all give a swell dress rehearsal! And you will!
    (General exclamations of relief.) Pick it up right
    after the scene!

The company rushes back to its places. Andy twitches
Marsh's sleeve.

227.   CLOSE-UP   ANDY AND MARSH

ANDY:
    Will he be able to go on tomorrow night?

MARSH (looking at Andy strangely; whispers quietly):
    He's dead. (Andy's jaw drops. Marsh turns away
    energetically.) Come on, folks, make it snappy!

(There is a faraway look in Marsh's eyes, but he tries not to let company see it.)

DISSOLVE TO:

228. FULL SHOT STAGE FROM AUDITORIUM
as full rehearsal of grand finale ends. Entire company is on stage with Dorothy in middle of front row.
The curtain falls with resounding crash of music from orchestra.

229. MED. SHOT UP AT STAGE
shooting past Marsh on feet in foreground.

MARSH (loudly):
Take it up!

Curtain rises again disclosing tired but happy company waiting apprehensively Marsh's words, fearing more rehearsal.

MARSH (grudgingly):
Not bad. That's all for tonight.

Ensemble reacts with relief.

MARSH (continuing; forcefully):
I want everybody to take their mind off the show. Go out and relax—forget it until ten o'clock tomorrow morning!

A spatter of applause and laughter.

MARSH (impressively):
I think it'll do. But I want you to be back here tomorrow to give the best performance you ever gave in your lives! Company dismissed.

ANDY (echoing importantly):
Comp'ny dismissed!

MAC (reechoing):
Company dismissed.

230.   FULL SHOT   STAGE

as company makes a break for dressing rooms with whoops of joy, the tension momentarily relaxed. Among those heading for the wings is Dorothy Brock, whose colored maid walks a few steps on stage to meet her with a cloak.

MAID:
   That wuz reely elegant—Mis' Brock.

DOROTHY (ignoring her compliment as she pulls cloak about her shoulders):
   Anybody phone, Pansy? (She asks it with feigned nonchalance.)

MAID:
   Phone? Oh, no, ma'am—no-buddy a-tall!

DOROTHY (frowning slightly as she walks toward wings):
   You're . . . sure?

MAID (very positively):
   Oh—ah certainly is . . . yes ma'am—Mis' Brock!

Compressing her lips, Dorothy disappears into wings.

231.   MED. SHOT   BACKSTAGE NEAR STAIRWAYS TO DRESSING
ROOMS

as members of company, stagehands, etc., scurry about gay and carefree. Billy intercepts Peggy hurrying past.

BILLY (tenderly):
   Hello—stranger . . . I've been trying to see you all evening . . .

PEGGY (a trifle hurt):
   Well—I haven't been off this stage since two o'clock today!

BILLY (ignoring her pointed thrust):
   I—I thought perhaps—you'd like to have some— supper with me . . .

PEGGY (somewhat icily):
> I would have, but I'm afraid you thought of it too late, Billy.

BILLY (weakly):
> I—I've been thinking of it all day long.

PEGGY (haughtily):
> Sorry—but I'm NOT a mind reader. I've got a date.

She turns from Billy, CAMERA PANNING with her as she starts down stairs.

232.   MED. SHOT   STAIRS
leading to chorus dressing room under stage as Peggy descends. Terry is waiting at the bottom of the stairs.

TERRY (cheerfully):
> Lissen, kid . . . I gotta run ahead an' get the stuff . . . mind? See you in 1061 at the hotel . . . and make it snappy!

Without waiting to see whether she minds or not, he makes a dash for the door.

PEGGY (sardonically):
> Just a great big bundle of good manners!

233.   FULL SHOT   EMPTY STAGE
Scenery, etc., cleared off stage, last stagehand slips on coat as he leaves.

Downstage center, by pilot light, in a kitchen chair, Marsh sits slumped down, hat brim down over eyes, thinking hard, cigarette dangling forgotten from lips.

DISSOLVE TO:

234.   CLOSE SHOT   MARSH
deep in thought. A burst of laughter off by stage entrance causes Marsh to raise head and look off.

235.   LONG SHOT TOWARD STAGE DOOR   FROM MARSH'S ANGLE
Lorraine joins Andy laughing at some crack of his. They turn toward exit.

236.   MED. SHOT ANDY AND LORRAINE
through doorway, Marsh in background on stage. Andy
is returning some unseen object to hip pocket, wiping
lips.

ANDY (feeling high, as he finishes a story):
. . . So the other guy says, "What do ya think *I* got
here—a DUCK!"

LORRAINE (shrieks):
AN-dee! You're TERR-ible! (She looks around furtively.) Do you know any more?

MARSH (raising hand and calling dispiritedly):
Andy!

Andy's face sobers suddenly. He quickly removes Lorraine's hand from his arm and steps away from her side
nervously.

LORRAINE (annoyed):
Go on—yes-man! Jump! Papa give you liver!

ANDY (hurriedly):
Don't BE like that. This may be important!

LORRAINE (with saccharine sweetness):
It CAN'T be—darling—he's calling YOU!

Andy, annoyed, hurries away and joins Marsh.

237.   MED. SHOT MARSH
as Andy enters to him. He evidences first signs of crack-
ing under the strain. He continues staring off wearily
into space as Andy joins him.

MARSH (without looking up):
Sit down, Andy.

Andy looks around vaguely for a place to sit, tips up a
switchbox, and squats on it impatiently. Marsh tosses
away his dead cigarette and lights a fresh one, coughing
as he gets it going. Andy looks off scene ruefully.

238.   LONG SHOT   LORRAINE IN DOORWAY
from Andy's angle. She beckons impatiently.

239.   CLOSE SHOT   ANDY
wringing hands. Looks off at Marsh hopefully.

240.   CLOSE-UP   MARSH FROM ANDY'S ANGLE
calmly smoking, mind busy.

241.   CLOSE SHOT   ANDY   FROM LORRAINE'S ANGLE
He looks back at Lorraine, shrugs hopelessly, a forlorn
face, jerking his head in Marsh's direction.

242.   MED. SHOT   LORRAINE   FROM ANDY'S ANGLE
as she waves hand in disgusted "good *night!*" and turns
away.

243.   MED. SHOT   ANDY AND MARSH
as Andy shakes head sadly and tries to make himself
comfortable waiting for Marsh to begin.
      Wearily, Marsh clears his throat; Andy looks at him
speculatively.

ANDY:
      Something wrong—chief?

MARSH (half smiles, ironically):
      Everything's wrong—Andy . . . My back's against
      the wall . . . I've cursed them—driven them—
      worn their feet off and torn their hearts out—who
      knows— (thinking of old trouper) I may even have
      killed one of them— Now they're calling me a
      devil—a slave driver . . . I guess they're right.

ANDY:
      You're a great director—Mr. Marsh.

MARSH:
      Maybe I WAS— Right now—I'm a *sick* man— They
      told me I was sick when I started—but I started

147

anyway—and Andy—I'm going to finish—and I'm going to have a show. Oh—I know what they'll say—They'll like it—They've GOT to—They'll say—"Marsh is a wizard—he turns 'em out like clockwork—the guy isn't human—he's a MA-CHINE!" (He shakes his head wearily.) I'm NOT a machine—Andy—and for the first time I'm counting on someone else—I've got to— I'm counting on YOU—and tomorrow night, Andy—we're going to give them a SHOW!

ANDY (with great feeling):
The best job Julian Marsh ever did!

DISSOLVE TO:

244.   EXT. MED. SHOT   STAGE ENTRANCE
Peggy hurries out alone. Pat suddenly steps up to her out of the shadows.

PAT (kiddingly):
Taxi?

PEGGY (in delighted surprise):
Why, Pat! What are you doing in Philadelphia?

PAT (chuckling):
I just got my passport and I thought I'd drop over.

PEGGY:
Business—? Or pleasure?

PAT:
I haven't found out yet—it's a *job!* (He steps up close to her and takes her arm.) How about one of those cozy midnight suppers you read so much about? I been hanging around here, hoping you'd come out.

PEGGY (regretfully):
Oh dear— I *have* a date . . .

PAT (persuasively):
Break it!

PEGGY:
I'd really like to—but I can't!

PAT:
You could—try.

PEGGY (shaking her head uncertainly):
You see—we open tomorrow night— It's with the company—and I really ought to be on hand.

PAT (accepting defeat gracefully):
I understand— Well, at least, let me drive you to the main event! (He looks off scene; taking her arm, he calls.) TAXI!

Abner and Dorothy come out of stage door. She is tired but elated. They walk toward curb.

245. FULL SHOT   ALONG SIDEWALK
Abner's car at curb; back of it cab hailed by Pat draws up to curb. Chauffeur opens door for Dorothy as cab stops by Pat and Peggy.

246. CLOSE-UP   DOROTHY
as she recognizes Pat, who does not see her. Her face becomes bleak, bitter.

247. FULL SHOT   TAXI AT CURB FROM DOROTHY'S ANGLE
as Pat very attentively hands Peggy into taxi. As taxi starts away, PAN with it (as if Dorothy's glance followed it). Pat is visibly leaning close to Peggy.

248. MED. SHOT   DOROTHY AT STEP OF LIMOUSINE
hurt and angry, with frown gets into car.

249. INT. CLOSE SHOT IN LIMOUSINE
Abner gets in beside Dorothy.

ABNER (to chauffeur):
Congress Hotel.

Door slams shut. Abner turns to Dorothy. She has closed her eyes, in apparent suffering. Abner is muchly concerned, as car starts.

ABNER (bordering between alarm and annoyance):
Y' ain't going to have another one of your spells—are yuh?

DOROTHY (looking at him sharply):
Spells? Oh—no—I'm tired. A rehearsal is no picnic.

ABNER:
A little party'll do you good.

DOROTHY (sourly):
I've BEEN done good!

ABNER:
Don't just bein' with me cheer you up?

DOROTHY (sarcastically):
Tremendously. I'm practically *hysterical* right now!

Dorothy leans back hopelessly with resigned shrug; her eyes are troubled, her mind on Pat.

DISSOLVE TO:

250. EXT. SIDEWALK BEFORE CONGRESS HOTEL   NIGHT
FULL SHOT
as taxi drives in and stops. Doorman opens door.

251. MED. SHOT   TAXICAB AT CURB
as Pat helps Peggy out.

PAT (holding her hand in a parting gesture):
This is the first taxi ride I've ever had . . . that wasn't too long!

PEGGY (sweetly):
You can say such nice things!

PAT (with mock modesty):
With the same inspiration—anybody could.

PEGGY (as her hand still in his, she starts to draw toward hotel):
I'm sorry about tonight.

PAT (sourly):
It's the tough Denning luck, I suppose.

PEGGY (smiling as she draws back):
Let's hope it changes!

PAT (succinctly):
It has! How about lunch tomorrow?

PEGGY:
No more dates till after we open . . . Good night, Pat, and thanks.

She enters the hotel and he reenters the waiting cab.

DISSOLVE TO:

252.   MED. SHOT   ANN AND MAN IN HOTEL ROOM
We see the man is Jones. A filled glass of champagne is shoved in under Ann's nose. The bubbles tickle her nose; she giggles inanely but seizes glass and raises it coyly.

JONES (gaily):
When I was a boy, they used to call THIS champagne!

ANN (drunkenly):
When you were a boy it used to BE champagne!

253.   FULL SHOT   DOROTHY'S SUITE
Gay drinking party at height. Folding "Tip Top" portable bar is set up, a male and female guest serving as amateur bartenders, aprons tied about waists. On table a tiny portable Victrola (expensive German type) blares popular tunes. Several couples dancing. Abner ambles about, the imperfect host.

254. CLOSE SHOT   DOROTHY AT BAR
moodily nursing a glass of champagne. She is thinking
of Pat and her nerves are on edge.

ABNER'S VOICE OFF (tipsily boisterous):
Give th' little boy a great big hand!

DIANA'S VOICE OFF:
Yeah . . . right across his great big mouth!

Dorothy glances in direction of voices, her face showing
distaste. Seizing another full glass of champagne, she
dodges approaching Abner and exits out of scene.

255. MED. SHOT   DOROTHY
passing deep lounge chair in which Barry sits with
flashy show girl sitting on arm of chair, glass in hand,
her other arm about his shoulder. Barry looks up at
Dorothy somewhat perturbed, as she downs drink and
lets Phillips refill her glass.

BARRY (in casual warning):
Another one o' those and they'll have to build a
bridge over you!

DOROTHY (belligerently):
And one more crack like that and they'll build a
monument over YOU!

BARRY (protesting):
But you gotta give a SHOW tomorrow—NOT an
exhibition!

DOROTHY (sullenly):
You'd never be able to tell that from the script!

She lurches away out of scene. Barry's eyes follow her,
increasingly worried. He pats show girl on leg.

BARRY:
Excuse me, lady, this is where you get off!

The show girl pouts as Barry disengages himself and rises. He hands her his glass. Immediately the girl smiles again. Barry goes. Girl empties one glass after another and slides plop off arm into seat of chair, smiling foolishly.

256. MED. SHOT DOROTHY
passing Abner without seeing him. He catches her arm.

ABNER (leering):
  'lo—Dotty!

Dorothy flings away from him. His jaw drops. CAMERA PANS with Dorothy as she moves on. She takes highball from hand of man who is arguing with a pretty girl, who keeps shaking her head. He looks after Dorothy, surprised, then shrugs. CAMERA PANS with Dorothy as she drops into chair and sips her drink, moodily tempestuous. Barry and Abner enter to her solicitously.

BARRY (anxiously):
  What's the matter with you tonight? (She glares at him.)

ABNER (plaintively):
  Yeah, Dorothy . . . you always treat me like this . . . You don't know how I feel . . .

DOROTHY (sarcastically, to Abner):
  If anybody does, I should!

BARRY (sarcastically, to Abner):
  In a star, it's temperament . . . In a chorus girl, it's bad taste!

DOROTHY (blazing suddenly):
  What is this? Target practice? Why can't you let me alone . . . wisecracking . . . heckling . . . complaining . . . finding fault . . . I'm sick of it . . . tired of you . . . all of you . . . do you hear?

She wheels angrily around, enters the bedroom, and slams the door.

BARRY (whistling softly, as he looks at Abner):
I'll bet the second verse is pretty!

257.   FULL SHOT   GROUP
near door, as the crowd reacts dumbfounded, alarmed. Barry steals worried look at Abner's flushed, irate countenance. Ann sways toward door, burlesquing Dorothy's action, and sidles up to Abner.

ANN (drunkenly):
Guess YOU'd better hop on your kiddie car and go on back to Cleveland . . . (She hiccups suddenly and, looking surprised, turns to Jones.) Excuse me . . . it's the tight shoes!

JONES (angrily):
Shut up!

Ann subsides.

258.   CLOSE SHOT AT DOOR
as Abner lumbers toward it.

BARRY:
Where ya going?

ABNER:
Mebbe little Dorothy needs me!

BARRY:
Go on, *don't* be a sucker for a crying act!

ABNER:
Me? Say, listen, Jones . . .

259.   INT. DOROTHY'S ROOM   CLOSE SHOT   DOROTHY
standing by small table near door, pouring self neat drink of whiskey.

ABNER'S VOICE OFF:
> One hundred thousand dollars is a lot to pay for a pack of insults . . . So that's what you been calling me behind my back . . . sucker, huh? Well, I ain't a sucker for anybody, see . . . Dorothy Brock don't mean that to me— (snaps fingers) if it hadn't been for me she wouldn'ta had a . . . show to star in! She better not try to give ME the air NOW!

Dorothy burns; blazing with indignation, she swings to door.

260.   MED. SHOT   LIVING ROOM AT DOOR
as Dorothy jerks it open and stands, glass in hand, facing Abner with flaming eyes. Abner shrivels beneath her scorn.

DOROTHY (harshly):
> So that's it—you small town big shot. I better not give you the air, huh? Well, that's exactly what I'm giving you right now!

She dashes contents of glass in Abner's face. Abner staggers back and all retreat toward hall door. Dorothy follows, hysterically shouting them out.

DOROTHY (fiercely):
> Get out—get out of my room!

ANN:
> This is no place for a person whose insurance ain't paid up!

Dorothy hurls glass after them as they dive for hall with excited babble of alarm. With a sweep of her arm she sends glasses crashing from top of bar. In a frenzy, as door closes after last of departing guests, Dorothy picks up Victrola and sends it hurtling in direction of door. Then she drops into a chair in a storm of furious weeping.

                                                    DISSOLVE TO:

261. CLOSE SHOT   MAN'S FEET IN ANOTHER HOTEL ROOM
as he kicks off slippers, sitting on edge of bed, and starts
to lift feet up into bed. Telephone rings off persistently.

PAT'S VOICE OFF:
Now, what!

Feet slip into slippers again and start off scene.

262. FULL SHOT   PAT'S ROOM
as he crosses angrily to phone.

263. CLOSE-UP   PAT AT PHONE

PAT:
Hello? (Face lights up in pleased surprise.) Dorothy!

264. CLOSE-UP   DOROTHY AT PHONE (IN HER ROOM)
She has been crying, is much wrought up. Her steady
drinking—a half-empty glass is in her hand—has made
her reckless.

DOROTHY (emotionally):
I can't go on with this, Pat! I've got to see you . . .
at once!

265. CLOSE-UP   PAT AT PHONE
frowning, puzzled and worried.

PAT:
But . . .

DOROTHY'S VOICE OVER WIRE (desperately):
Please, Pat, please! Don't ask me why—just
come—now!

PAT:
Of course, dear. I'll be right over.

He hangs up.

266. FULL SHOT PAT'S ROOM
as he rises, crosses decisively to closet, gets clothes, and
starts to dress.

DISSOLVE TO:

267. CLOSE SHOT MARSH IN BED
sitting up in lounging pajamas, working. Inevitable
cigarette dangles from lips, face drawn, shadows under
eyes, still unshaven, hair unkempt. Counterpane
strewn with papers, music cue sheets, plans, etc. Drink
is handy on night table, which is a welter of cigarette
butts.

Marsh looks up off scene impatiently. Pushes papers
viciously aside.

Secretary opens door to sitting room and gestures to
someone off, as Marsh irritably crushes out cigarette.
Jones, Barry, and Abner bustle in excitedly. Secretary
goes out, closes door after him.

MARSH:
What's up?

His questioning glance goes from Barry to Jones, both
shrug hopelessly with nod at Abner, who lumbers angrily toward Marsh.

ABNER (boiling over with pent-up fury):
Dorothy's out of the show! (Marsh frowns.)
Definitely—once 'n—for all—she's OUT!

MARSH (contemptuously):
Well, let me have it. What happened?

ABNER (boiling over):
She THREW me out of her room, that's what!

MARSH (harshly; interrupting):
And now you want to throw HER out. What is this
. . . a game? (Throws back covers, swings feet to
floor, sits on edge of bed, and shakes a warning
finger at Abner.) You can't do it!

157

ABNER (bristling):
>   Oh, no?

MARSH (with finality; standing up):
>   Brock's in my show to stay . . . and THAT'S final!

ABNER:
>   If Dorothy stays *in*, my dough comes *out*! And *that's*
>   final! (Turns away, puffing angrily.)

268.   CLOSE SHOT   ABNER AND MARSH
as Marsh catches lapels and swings Abner round
fiercely, so they are face to face.

MARSH:
>   Why you pot-bellied sap! You've got seventy
>   thousand dollars SUNK in this show already. Are
>   you gonna just toss that away—because of a
>   dame—*any* dame?

ABNER:
>   That's my funeral, ain't it?

MARSH:
>   Yes . . . and the funeral of two hundred other
>   people besides . . . Chorus girls, boys, electricians.
>   You wouldn't be that small, would you?

Abner, suddenly calmer, squirms uneasily, and rubs his
chin thoughtfully.

ABNER:
>   Well, I—well, she threw ME out! I think she ought
>   to apologize.

MARSH:
>   Of course she'll apologize. Brock isn't like that—
>   She'll be sorry—by morning. Don't take it like that,
>   Mr. Dillon. Why, do you know that back in New
>   York they're calling you the angel of Broadway?

ABNER (grinning fatuously):
> Are they? Um. Well, I guess maybe if she apologizes . . . I can overlook it. But it must be *tonight*. That's final.

Abner exits. Three men look at each other. Jones gets an idea, grabs newspaper from table, opens it excitedly.

269.   INSERT CLOSE-UP NEWSPAPER THEATRICAL PAGE
An advertisement which reads:

ARCH STREET THEATER
PREMIERE TONIGHT
DOROTHY BROCK
in
"PRETTY LADY"

Next to it advertisement reads:

"STRAND THEATER"
OPENING NEXT MONDAY
WM. PENN PLAYERS
in
"SAVE THE PIECES!"
with
RUTH COLLINGS   PAT DENNING
Geoffrey Waring
Lora Carewe

Jones's finger underscores Pat's name.

JONES'S VOICE ⌣ (bitterly):
> There's your answer, Julian! That Denning guy is IN again!

BACK TO SCENE:

270.   FULL SHOT ROOM
as Marsh disgustedly slams paper down on table, snarling at Jones, striding up and down in a frenzy.

MARSH:
> Get down to her room—quick! Wait outside—if Denning is there, phone me! I'll dress and come right down!

JONES (alarmed, protesting):
 But—Julian—

MARSH (interrupting harshly):
 The show's going on! If that guy's mixing in my affairs again—I'll break his dirty neck. Hurry up!

Marsh gestures Jones out as he starts to rip off lounging robe and reaches for his trousers.

DISSOLVE TO:

271.   MED. SHOT   TERRY AND PEGGY AT PARTY IN TERRY'S ROOM
The room is full of "drunk-and-disorderlies"—show girls, chorus girls, chorus boys, and the lower social order from the show. A radio rings out a popular jazz tune and some couples dance. Others neck, stagger around, and ad lib. Peggy, disconcerted, a drink in her hand, walks a few steps to a table, places her drink on the table edge, and looking furtively around is about to walk away from it when Terry suddenly comes on scene and grabs her by the arm.

TERRY (attempting to take her in his arms):
 'Smatter—baby . . . say . . . you ain't warmin' up a-tall!

PEGGY (trying to avoid him):
 Don't . . . Terry . . . Please . . .

TERRY (drunkenly):
 Aw—come on—that ain't no way to act . . .

PEGGY:
 Listen, Terry—you have me wrong! I'm NOT acting . . . (She squirms but he tightens his grip.) I—just—don't—like to be pawed . . .

TERRY (with mock sincerity):
 Aw . . . honey . . .

As Peggy struggles to free herself, the lights go out suddenly and there is a chorus of exclamations, synthetic "kiss smacks," and much suggestive laughter.

MAN'S VOICE (with feigned regret):
Oh—oh—musta been a fuse!

GIRL'S VOICE (tipsily):
Yeah—a fuse named CHARLIE!

There is a loud smack as we hear

TERRY'S VOICE:
Why you . . .

And the lights snap on again suddenly to show Terry feeling his face where Peggy slapped him and starting drunkenly for Peggy, who is making for the door.

272. LONG SHOT   HOTEL CORRIDOR
shooting down hall past elevators toward door of Terry's room as Peggy comes out, stands momentarily undecided, then hurries down hall toward elevators and CAMERA.

TERRY'S VOICE OFF (calling angrily):
Peggy! Where are ya! Come back!

Peggy dodges into chambermaid's broom closet just as Terry rushes into hall and staggers down hall toward elevators past her hiding place.

273. FULL SHOT   CORRIDOR   REVERSE ANGLE
as Terry presses furiously at elevator bell. Peggy peeks out of hiding place in foreground, sees that stairs are between her and Terry. Stealthily she steals to head of stairs while Terry is absorbed in calling elevator, and dashes down the stairs.

274. FULL SHOT   CORRIDOR   FLOOR BELOW
shooting past elevators toward stairs as Peggy comes down, starts toward elevators, pauses, shrugs whimsically, and starts on down stairs.

DISSOLVE TO:

275.   FULL SHOT   CORRIDOR   THIRD FLOOR
Stairway in foreground, elevators beyond and down
hall, beyond a hallway leading off at right angles, the
door of Dorothy's suite (304–6–8). Peggy wearily descends to corridor, turns to go on down when elevator
door opens. Peggy, thinking it's Terry after her, draws
back against wall watching. Pat emerges from elevator
and starts away from Peggy down hall.

276.   CLOSE-UP   PEGGY
as she recognizes Pat, reacts, and starts out after him.

277.   MED. SHOT   CORRIDOR   TOWARD DOROTHY'S SUITE
from Peggy's angle as Pat approaches door, CAMERA
TRUCKING after him. He pauses at door, raps lightly,
door is opened by Dorothy who greets Pat affectionately
and draws him inside room, closing door. We see room
number 304.

278.   MED. SHOT   PEGGY
reacting, standing near corner of hallway, leading off
main corridor. She starts suddenly at sound of someone
inside hallway and backs up to closed door, watching.

279.   FULL SHOT   CORRIDOR TOWARD DOROTHY'S SUITE (FROM
PEGGY'S ANGLE)
as Jones comes from side hall and sneaks stealthily up to
Dorothy's door. He listens at door, hesitates, decides it
is safer not to throw Pat out. Then hastily turns and
hurries decisively toward elevator to summon Marsh.

280.   CLOSE SHOT   PEGGY
alarmed at sight of Jones, bends over close to door as if
having trouble with lock, apparently about to enter
room. Her face is hidden as Jones hurries past paying no
attention to her.

281.   FULL SHOT   CORRIDOR

Peggy is in foreground at door as Jones rings elevator bell, then, impatient of delay, hurries up stairway. Peggy straightens up and starts purposefully toward CAMERA.

282.   CLOSE SHOT   DOOR OF DOROTHY'S SUITE (304)

as Peggy enters, stands undecided for a moment, then resolutely knocks at door. There is no answer and Peggy knocks again imperatively.

Dorothy opens the door with assumed arrogant innocence; she is feeling her liquor.

PEGGY (excitedly):
    Miss Brock—Pat—I saw—

DOROTHY (recognizing Peggy, furious):
    I'm just beginning to see, you little sneak!

PEGGY:
    What do you mean?

DOROTHY:
    How dare you spy on us?

Pat appears at Dorothy's side as Peggy prevents her closing the door again.

PEGGY (earnestly):
    Spying! I wasn't spying— I just wanted to tell you—

PAT:
    Peggy!

DOROTHY (wildly):
    I know! You're jealous . . . you've been after him yourself . . .

Pat tries to quiet Dorothy, pulling her from door. Peggy pushes inside.

283.   MED. SHOT   DOROTHY'S LIVING ROOM
shooting toward hall door as Peggy closes and stands against it. Pat tries to hold and quiet Dorothy, who is wild with rage.

PEGGY (excitedly):
Pat . . . there's going to be trouble . . . you . . .

PAT (stepping forward):
Wait a minute, Dorothy! Let's see what this is all about.

DOROTHY (working herself into a pitch):
Wait a minute . . . for what . . . more spying . . . more double-crossing . . . I won't wait . . . Let me go! (She screams now.) Let me go!

She tears herself from Pat's hold and, lurching toward Peggy, trips over the Victrola, lying on the floor where she threw it earlier.[19] She stumbles in a blind rage, falls, and knocks over a chair, screaming with pain and bursting into tears as her leg twists under her.

284.   CLOSE SHOT   DOROTHY ON FLOOR
as Pat and Peggy bend over her. Dorothy's face suddenly goes white and she passes out cold.

PEGGY (quickly):
It's her ankle.

Pat starts to lift unconscious Dorothy in his arms.

285.   FULL SHOT   DOROTHY'S LIVING ROOM
still showing wreckage of earlier party. Pat carries Dorothy rapidly toward bedroom door, Peggy assisting, worried.

DISSOLVE TO:

286.   CLOSE SHOT   DOROTHY ON BED
as Pat and Peggy bend over her. Peggy feels her ankle as Pat chafes her hands.

PEGGY (ominously):
  It's swelling!

Pat, alarmed, starts out. Peggy stares down at Dorothy, then hurries to bathroom.

287. CLOSE SHOT   LIVING ROOM   PAT AT PHONE
PAT:
  Get me the house physician!

288. MED. SHOT   BEDROOM
Peggy hurries back from bathroom with smelling salts and wet towel. Bends over unconscious Dorothy.

289. FULL SHOT   LIVING ROOM
Pat hangs up and starts back to bedroom as hall door bursts open; Marsh enters and sees Pat going toward bedroom.

MARSH (harshly):
  Wait a minute, you!

Pat turns, surprised. Marsh strides over to him.

290. CLOSE SHOT   PAT
as Marsh enters to him. Marsh's eyes blaze with indignation, his hands clench.

MARSH (snarling, authoritative):
  I want to talk to you!
PAT:
  There's no time—
MARSH (catching his shoulder):
  You listen to me—
PAT (excitedly):
  Wait a minute! (He jerks his head toward bedroom.)
  She's hurt . . . pretty badly, too . . . her ankle
  . . . may be broken . . .

Marsh, thunderstruck, pushes past Pat into bedroom.

291.   FULL SHOT   AT BED
as Marsh hurries in, followed by Pat. Marsh ignores
Peggy, who is bathing Dorothy's forehead, a scared look
on her face. He takes a look at Dorothy, sniffs, and nods
angrily, realizing she'd been drinking.

MARSH:
    Which one?

Pat indicates ankle. Marsh grasps ankle and twists it.[20]
Dorothy's body winces.

MARSH (looks at Pat and Peggy):
    Broken? (Peggy half nods.)

PEGGY:
    I'm afraid—

MARSH (interrupting brutally):
    You're not sure, are you? (Peggy shakes her head.)
    It may be just a sprain!

                                        DISSOLVE TO:

292.   FULL SHOT   AT BED
doctor bending over Dorothy's ankle making examination. Peggy stands at head of bed. Marsh near doctor.
Marsh turns impatiently, noticing Peggy's anxious face.

MARSH (sharply, to Peggy):
    Well, what are you standing there for . . . ? Get a
    glass of water for Miss Brock . . .

PEGGY (nervously):
    Oh—yes, sir . . . I thought . . .

MARSH (impatiently):
    I'll do the thinking for both of us. Move, now.

Peggy scurries out of scene. Doctor looks up, his face
serious.

DOCTOR (to Marsh, with curt nod):
    Compound fracture.

166

Marsh grunts and without a word walks moodily out of bedroom.

293.   MED. SHOT   LIVING ROOM
Pat, seated by bedroom door, raises his head inquiringly.

MARSH (answering Pat's questioning look):
Broken, all right. (He continues toward door, stops suddenly, and swings around upon Pat accusingly.) I still don't know what *you*'re doing here!

PAT (angrily, as he rises):
If I thought it was any of your business, I'd tell you.

Marsh stares sullenly at Pat for a second, grits his teeth, exits to door, turns, and looks back:

MARSH:
Too bad it wasn't her neck!

FADE OUT

FADE IN
294.   FULL SHOT   BACKSTAGE   MORNING
Company assembled apprehensively, whispering rumors, nervous, waiting Marsh's arrival. Marsh, his face hard and cold, stalks in followed by Barry, and faces company. There is dead silence as they await his words.

MARSH (cryptically; he looks slowly around the group before him, before he speaks, then clears his throat, and speaks without emotion, wearily):
Our star . . . Miss Brock . . . has had an accident. She has broken her ankle. There will be no performance tonight. (There is a general gasp of dismay, as CAMERA QUICKLY PANS around group, registering expressions.) Wait a minute. Quiet, please. You will NOT leave the theater until you are officially dismissed. (He wheels around to Andy.) Get

that, Andy. You're to hold the company here for further instructions.

ANDY'S VOICE OFF:
Righto. (To company.) All of you, now . . . stick around!

MAC (echoing):
Everybody stick around!

Marsh turns on heel and exits toward dressing rooms. As he goes, company bursts into excited babble of worry and alarm.

295.   MED. SHOT   ANDY AND MEMBERS OF COMPANY
Andy drops on chair by table shaking head in despair, looks up, and sees Lorraine and Peggy with long faces standing nearby.

LORRAINE (with a sour grimace):
Well, that's Africa!

PEGGY:
You mean there's not going to be a . . . show? (She's almost on the verge of tears.)

LORRAINE:
How you do catch on! That's the idea!

PEGGY (appealingly to Andy):
But we've rehearsed . . . for five weeks . . .

ANDY (authoritatively):
That's show business. Here today . . . and here tomorrow! You don't make much money, but you get a lotta exercise.

PEGGY (thinking of her finances):
But . . . but . . . even a chorus girl has to LIVE!

LORRAINE:
Says who?

296. FULL SHOT   DRESSING ROOM
converted into temporary office for Marsh. Marsh paces,
smoking furiously at cigarette. Barry sits disconsolately,
head in hands. Door bursts open, Jones bounces in, all
excitement.

JONES (bubbling over):
> Listen . . . Dillon just phoned . . . He's got every-
> thing fixed . . .

MARSH (cynically):
> Up to and including Brock's ankle, I suppose.

JONES (excitedly):
> No . . . don't you understand . . . He's going
> through with it . . .

BARRY (glumly):
> How?

JONES:
> I tell you . . . he's found somebody to take Brock's
> place . . . He's on his way over here with her now!

The three men rise, with a sudden single impulse, and
rush pell-mell for the door.

MARSH (plaintively hopeful):
> And after all those things I've been thinking about
> him . . . too!

DISSOLVE TO:

297. EXT. FULL SHOT   AT STAGE DOOR
Marsh, Barry, and Jones looking off eagerly anxious.
Andy and Mac behind them.

298. EXT. FULL SHOT   STAGE DOOR ALLEY   REVERSE ANGLE
FROM STAGE DOOR
Abner's limousine pulls up and stops. Chauffeur hops
down, opens door.

299.   EXT. CLOSE SHOT   LIMOUSINE DOOR
Abner's bulky rear end appears in door and he backs out
onto ground. He turns, a seraphic smile on his face; in
his arm gingerly he holds Fifi, the Peke. He extends his
hand into car and helps Ann to alight in all her ritzy
glory.

ANN (bestowing a languishing smile on Abner and nods
toward car):
Thanks, Abbie! Now there's a kiddie car I could go
for!

300.   EXT. CLOSE SHOT   AT STAGE DOOR
as Marsh, Barry, and Jones recognize Ann and gasp in
amazed despair. They exchange glances. Marsh groans.
Andy winks at Mac.

ANDY (under his breath):
"Anytime Annie!" Well lay me low!

301.   EXT. MED. SHOT   STAGE DOOR
as Abner and Ann reach steps before Marsh and others.

ABNER (beaming with fatuous contentment):
Your new leading lady, folks. I guess I saved the
day all right this time!

MARSH (without enthusiasm):
Let's go inside and talk it over.

The group starts inside, Barry's and Jones's faces a
study, Ann nodding to one and all with great conde-
scension.

DISSOLVE TO:

302.   INT. FULL SHOT   DRESSING ROOM OFFICE
Ann sits coyly center, Barry and Jones droop disconsolately by door. Abner, all smiles, has eyes only for his
gorgeous gal. Marsh, hard eyed and grim lipped, stands
over Ann.

MARSH (forcefully, but with great tact):
There's a big investment in this show so far, Dillon . . .

ANN (flippantly, looking at Abner):
Huh—YOU'RE telling HIM!

MARSH (ignoring her, and continuing to address Abner):
And while I appreciate your trying to help, I'm afraid this young woman won't . . .

ABNER (butting in enthusiastically):
Sure she will. At first she didn't want to, but I convinced her . . . got her all set . . . she'll be sensational . . .

ANN (rising and grimacing dryly):
How about letting *me* talk, huh?

She waves Abner away imperiously. Puzzled, he starts to say something, swallows, and changes his mind.

ABNER (looking at the others):
Well, all right, my dear . . .

303. CLOSE SHOT ANN, MARSH, ABNER

ANN (to Marsh, frankly herself):
Let's quit kiddin', Mr. Marsh. (To Abner.) Abbie, all those promises sounded swell—at breakfast— (Abner chokes guiltily, Marsh looks at him in amused understanding.) but I haven't got a chance of carryin' this show— (To Marsh.) I know that as well as you do, maybe better![21]

MARSH (dryly, nods):
I appreciate your honesty.

ANN (earnestly):
That's swell—cause listen: You got somebody in this outfit who *can* carry your show— (Marsh looks at her sharply) a great little trouper—honest, Mr. Marsh!

MARSH:

Don't you think I'm capable of selecting—

ANN (interrupting):

Sure—but you'd never pick this one—and I'm telling you she can swing it! (Marsh frowns impatiently.) How can you lose? All you gotta do is try her!

MARSH (impressed by her sincerity):

Who?

ANN:

Sawyer!

MARSH:

Sawyer?

ANN:

Yes, Peggy Sawyer! Her voice may not panic 'em, but she can dance rings around Brock! Your show's half dancing, anyway. She'd kill 'em, I mean it!

ABNER:

But—darling—

ANN (firmly):

Outside!

MARSH (mulling it over):

But Sawyer— Nobody ever heard of her—just a raw kid—out of the chorus.

ANN (pleading earnestly):

Listen, Mister Marsh, I been workin' years for a chance like this. If I turn it down for somebody else—*believe* me, she's *gotta* be good!

MARSH (playing hunch):

Send her in.

Barry dodges out door.

BARRY'S VOICE OFF (calling):
Mac! Mac! Get Sawyer!

Ann turns to disappointed Abner.

ANN (wearily):
Well, now that that's over, Daddy, let's go out and
lean against a steak!

ABNER (patting her hand, emotionstruck):
Well I'll be—

ANN (grins at him):
Sure you will—but do you have to broadcast it!

304.   FULL SHOT   DRESSING ROOM OFFICE
as Barry ushers nervous Peggy in. Marsh looks her over
fiercely.

MARSH (grunts):
Humph! Experience?

PEGGY (a little, scared voice):
Just—just this show, Mr. Marsh.

MARSH (seeing possibilities):
Know the songs—dance routines? (Peggy nods.)
Think you could play the lead tonight?

PEGGY (gasping, big eyed):
The—*lead?*

ANN (encouragingly):
'Course ya can, Peggy! Don't let 'em scare ya!

MARSH (galvanized into activity):
All right—I'll give you a trial! (He shrugs.) I'll have
to!

There is a flurry of excitement in the room.

MARSH (hustling them all out):
Out of here—all of you! Send in Jerry—and close
that door! I don't want anybody in here for the next

five hours. I'll either have a live leading woman—or a dead chorus girl. (The door closes; to Peggy.) Now!

DISSOLVE TO:

305.　CLOSE SHOT　MARSH AND PEGGY

both seated. Marsh, coatless and disheveled, holds script in hand. Peggy reading a line. She is tired and nervous.

PEGGY (flatly):
"Jim. They didn't tell me you were here. It was grand of you to come."

MARSH (snarling):
No! That's impossible! You're greeting the man you love! It's your entrance speech! Make it *mean* something. Listen: (Putting life into it.) "Jim! They didn't tell me *you* were here. It was *grand* of you to come!" (Peggy nods.) Try it again!

PEGGY (with meaning):
"Jim! They didn't tell me *you* were here. It was *grand* of you to come!"

MARSH (grudging approval):
That's better. Let me hear the next.

Peggy goes at it earnestly.

DISSOLVE TO:

306.　FULL SHOT　MARSH AND PEGGY AND PIANIST IN DRESSING ROOM OFFICE

Pianist batting out music of duet. Peggy stands wringing her hands, trying her best. Marsh, a maniac, glares at her as he paces the room.

PEGGY (breaking off miserably):
I can't—I can't!

MARSH (brutally):
You can't, but you *will!*

174

PEGGY:
> Please, Mr. Marsh . . .

MARSH:
> Do you want this chance—or don't you?

PEGGY (grits teeth doggedly):
> Let's go over it again. I'll try!

Pianist starts again. Peggy attacks the song once more.

DISSOLVE TO:

307. FULL SHOT   DRESSING ROOM OFFICE
Peggy at end of tap routine. Marsh hunched in foreground watching avidly. Floor littered with cigarette butts. Peggy finishes breathlessly, hoping for some praise.

MARSH (somberly, without moving):
> Fair, only fair!

She drops in chair, exhausted. Marsh with shaking fingers lights new cigarette. There is a knock on the door.

MARSH (harshly):
> Well?

MAC'S VOICE OFF:
> One hour to curtain time, Chief!

MARSH (a grunt):
> Right! (Jerking thumb at pianist.) Outside!

Pianist exits. Marsh turns to Peggy.

308. CLOSE SHOT   PEGGY IN CHAIR   MARSH STANDING OVER HER
Marsh grips her savagely by shoulders.

MARSH (harshly):
> Listen, Sawyer—you let me down—and I'll—
> (Catching himself, he shrugs, softening, and points

175

to couch.) Lie down! Relax! I'll call you in time! The wardrobe women will have to come in to fit your costumes, but rest all you can. You're definitely going on tonight!

He turns sharply and goes out. Peggy rises as in a dream and crosses dazed toward couch.

309.   MED. SHOT   OUTSIDE DOOR OF DRESSING ROOM OFFICE
Barry, Jones, Mac, etc., waiting outside as Marsh, bleary eyed from tension, staggers out. Barry and Jones jump forward anxiously.

BARRY AND JONES (together):
   Julian—? Well—?

MARSH (blinking at them):
   The show goes on! (A flash of his old energy.) Wardrobe everybody!

Barry, Jones, and the others scurry away. Marsh turns away toward another dressing room, coming face to face with Billy, who stands with tray of coffee, looking very worried. Billy starts toward door where Peggy is. Marsh halts him.

MARSH (snarling viciously):
   Where you going?

BILLY:
   Coffee—Mr. Marsh—for—for Peggy. I guess maybe she needs it!

Marsh regards Billy quizzically; his glance shifts to door and back to Billy. Marsh knows people. There is a twinkle in his tired eyes; he grunts.

MARSH (dryly cynical):
   She needs a lot! (He jerks his head toward door.) Go on—and see that nobody else bothers her—or talks to her. *Nobody*—understand? (Billy nods.)

Marsh turns on heel and stumbles into another dressing room. Billy steps to door and taps on it.

PEGGY'S VOICE OFF (quavery with excitement):
Come in.

Billy steps inside.

310.   FULL SHOT   DRESSING ROOM OFFICE
Peggy sits upon couch, looking wide eyed and afraid at door as Billy enters and puts tray on make-up shelf.

PEGGY (with a sigh of relief):
Billy!

311.   CLOSE SHOT   PEGGY ON COUCH
as Billy brings her coffee.

BILLY:
Coffee—I guess maybe you can use it!

PEGGY (taking cup, chattering excitedly):
Oh, Billy—I'm so excited I think maybe I'm dreaming!

BILLY (shakes head):
You're awake all right—

PEGGY (suddenly frightened, whispering):
Billy—what—what's going to happen to me?

BILLY (shakes head):
You'll knock 'em cold, Peggy—you'll be the biggest thing that ever hit Broadway!

PEGGY (starry eyed, hopeful):
Gosh, Billy—I hope so!

BILLY (nods):
I know it. And I'm for you—you know that—even if— (He breaks off.)

PEGGY:
If what?

312.   CLOSE-UP   BILLY
not meeting Peggy's eyes.

BILLY (faltering):
> Listen, honey . . . I've been for you ever since the
> day you walked in on me in my B.V.D.'s. I've been
> wanting to tell you—almost from the start—how I
> feel about you— Gee, Peggy—I just don't know
> how to say it—but you DO know what I mean—
> don't you . . .

PEGGY'S VOICE OFF:
> But Billy . . . you and . . .

BILLY:
> I—I guess it sounds funny—the way I say it—but—
> the lines are new—for me—offstage . . .

PEGGY'S VOICE OFF:
> I guess—maybe—I can read between the lines . . .
> Billy . . . but I—want to hear you say it—say . . .
> some more . . .

BILLY:
> Peggy—I'm— (He starts up suddenly, as he hears
> someone at the door.)

313.   FULL SHOT   DRESSING ROOM OFFICE
Billy starts for door. Peggy jumps to her feet to stop him,
as the door opens, revealing Dorothy on crutches.

314.   CLOSE SHOT   AT DOORWAY
Dorothy stands there on crutches, pale faced, sunken
eyed, tight lipped—a figure of menace. She makes her
way into room slowly, never taking her burning eyes
from Peggy.

DOROTHY (in metallic, cold voice):
> They said—you were—in here.

315.   FULL SHOT   PEGGY, DOROTHY, AND BILLY
Peggy and Billy stare in alarm. Dorothy's expression
does not change.

PEGGY (awkwardly):
   Miss Brock—I—

BILLY (coming to life):
   You can't talk to her—nobody can—Marsh's orders!

DOROTHY (staring at Billy):
   I've things to say to her. Now leave us alone, Billy!

BILLY:
   But— (He looks at Peggy.)

Peggy, not knowing what to expect, spunkily declines
to show her fear. She nods at Billy, forcing a smile.

PEGGY (tremulously):
   It's all right, Billy.

With another look at Dorothy, Billy goes out uncomfortably.
   Dorothy and Peggy stare at each other for a long second. Dorothy sinks onto chair, leaning crutches against
shelf.

316.   CLOSE SHOT   DOROTHY   FROM PEGGY'S ANGLE
sitting in chair studying Peggy, off.

DOROTHY (in strange voice):
   So—you're going to take *my* place.

317.   CLOSE-UP   PEGGY
Her face suddenly sympathetic.

PEGGY (sincerely):
   I—I'm sorry!

318.   CLOSE SHOT   DOROTHY

DOROTHY (crisply):
>   What for? (A smile twists at her mouth.) It's your
>   chance, isn't it?

319.   CLOSE-UP   PEGGY
tears springing to her eyes, her face lovely and scared,
trying to smile.

PEGGY (simply):
>   But it's tough—on you!

320.   CLOSE SHOT   DOROTHY
stretching out her arm.

DOROTHY:
>   Come here—Peggy, isn't it?

Peggy nods, comes closer to Dorothy.

DOROTHY (understandingly now):
>   Listen to me— When I started for here tonight—I
>   was going to tear your heart out. And then I got to
>   thinking. I've had my chance—now it's your turn.
>   You want fame—well, you'll probably get it. And
>   why not? I've had enough. For five years it's kept
>   me away from the only thing I've ever wanted and,
>   funny thing, it was a broken ankle that helped me
>   find it out. That's why I'm not burnt up or resent-
>   ful. (Scornfully.) A career? Anybody can have
>   one—with the right breaks. As for me—I'll take Pat,
>   and vaudeville, or whatever goes with him. We're
>   being married—tomorrow.[22]

Peggy impulsively takes Dorothy's hands in hers. There
is a knock at the door.

PEGGY:
>   Come in.

321. FULL SHOT ROOM
as wardrobe woman enters with armful of costumes.

WARDROBE WOMAN:
We gotta hurry, miss! Stand right here.

Peggy gives herself into hands of wardrobe woman. Dorothy sits watching as Peggy slips into costume.

DISSOLVE TO:

322. FULL SHOT ROOM
Dorothy, Peggy, wardrobe woman relatively in same position but Peggy now is in costume, made-up, radiantly lovely. She is ready to go on. Wardrobe woman steps back, surveys her handiwork, clucks approvingly. Dorothy calls Peggy to her, takes her hands.

DOROTHY:
You look gorgeous! I'm going to wish you only one thing, my dear. Go out there—and be so swell you'll make me hate you!

Peggy starts toward door. Dorothy watching her approvingly.

DISSOLVE TO:

323. FULL SHOT IN WINGS
Members of company in costume and make-up, stagehands, etc., are scurrying about. Marsh stands grimly waiting. Orchestra starts playing off.

DISTANT VOICE OFF:
Overture! Overture!

Marsh comes to life, claps hands.

MARSH (sharply):
When she comes out, I don't want anyone to speak to her, NOT ANYONE!

Heads turn suddenly toward dressing room. Peggy in costume approaches like one in a dream.

MARSH (harshly):
Here she is—now break up!

Company moves away quickly, nervously. Peggy, breathing quickly, comes straight to Marsh. He takes her by the arm and steps with her close to wings, without a word.

324. CLOSE SHOT   MARSH AND PEGGY IN WINGS
shooting toward stage. Peggy shivers. Marsh tightens his grip on her arm.

MARSH (growling):
Steady! Steady!

The curtain rises. The music swells louder. We see beyond Marsh and Peggy the lights hit the chorus in its opening number. Peggy stiffens, her chin comes up. Marsh turns to her, speaking with tremendous force.

MARSH:
Now listen to me—listen hard. (With increasing intensity.) Two hundred people—two hundred jobs—two hundred thousand dollars—five weeks of grind—and blood and sweat—depend on you. It's the life of all these people who have worked with you. You've got to go on—and you've got to give—and give and give—they've GOT to like you—GOT to—you understand— (Beads of sweat stand out on his forehead now.) You can't fall down—you *can't*— Your future's in it—my future's in it—and everything that all of us have is staked on you— I'm through— Now keep your feet on the ground—and your head on those shoulders of yours—and go out—and Sawyer—you're going out a youngster—you've GOT to come back a star! [23] (He breaks off, looks at her intently, stiffens, clutches her to him fiercely for a split second.) There's your cue!

He pushes her brutally out into the spot.

325.   FULL SHOT   AUDITORIUM FROM PEGGY'S ANGLE
Glare of lights. Immense sea of gleaming faces wavering
through mist of spotlight rays.

326.   CLOSE-UP   PEGGY ON STAGE
reacting to smash of lights and audience. She blinks,
takes deep breath, and speaks—giving the line more
than in rehearsal. As she approaches leading man.

PEGGY (her voice strong, clear, vibrant):
Jim! They didn't tell me *you* were here! It was *grand*
of you to come! (She flashes her brilliant, appealing
smile.)

327.   FLASH   CLOSE-UP   MARSH
straining forward in wings, staring, tense, tearing
cigarette to pieces, worried, moving with every move
that Peggy makes.

328.   FLASH   CLOSE-UP   ANDY AND MAC
staring, worried. Andy, chewing gum hard; Mac, biting
on ragged cigar.

329.   FLASH   CLOSE-UP   ANN AND LORRAINE
gaping entranced at their pal. They exchange meaning-
ful glances. Ann winks elaborately.

330.   FLASH   CLOSE-UP   BILLY
apprehensively frowning as he watches. A smile begins
to brighten his face.

331.   FLASH   CLOSE-UP   DOROTHY
her eyes big with apprehension, breathing hard.

332.   FLASH   FULL SHOT   STAGE   FROM AUDIENCE
as Peggy and leading man reach cue for their number.

333. FLASH MED. SHOT ORCHESTRA LEADER
and nearest musicians, all in immaculately full dress.
Leader taps baton on music stand and orchestra starts
introduction.

334. CLOSE SHOT PEGGY AND LEADING MAN
She gives him tremulous look; he gives her an encourag-
ing firm handclasp and approving nod of head. Music
goes into verse. Peggy and leading man go into their
duet.

335. FLASH MED. SHOT BACKSTAGE RIGHT
Andy, very excited, lining up chorus girls for their entrance. Duet heard off.

336. FLASH MED. SHOT BACK STAGE LEFT
Mac lining up chorus boys for their entrance. Duet off.

337. LONG SHOT PEGGY AND LEADING MAN FROM DOROTHY'S
ANGLE
doing their stuff.

338. MED. SHOT DOROTHY
as Marsh, nervously pacing about, never taking eyes
from stage, comes up behind her. He is increasingly
confident but still tense. His hand unconsciously grips
Dorothy's shoulder, though he has not noticed her.
Dorothy looks up, smiling slow, rueful smile as she
notes Marsh's preoccupation, raises her hand and pats
his as it rests on her shoulder. Marsh looks down, surprised. They exchange understanding smiles. He pats
her shoulder sympathetically.

339. FULL SHOT STAGE FROM AUDIENCE ANGLE
Peggy and leading man start chorus of duet, as chorus
boys and girls enter for number. Chorus backs up Peggy
and leading man to finish of number. They head for
wings.

340. FULL SHOT   AUDIENCE
bursting into spontaneous, hearty applause.

341. FULL SHOT   MARSH, ETC. IN WINGS
as Peggy and leading man enter from stage at end of
number, panting, breathless.
Marsh grabs Peggy. She looks at Marsh fearfully,
questioning. Marsh turns to company, gathering up.

MARSH (harshly):
Get back—everybody!

He leads Peggy to dressing room door, CAMERA TRUCK-
ING with them through crowd.

MARSH (gruffly):
Good girl—you got by. But you're not finished yet.
The toughest part's coming and you can't be a flash
in the pan. We're back of you—everybody in the
house—and there isn't an actor on that stage who
doesn't know what you're up against—who isn't
pulling for you. (He takes her by the shoulders,
looks hard into her eyes, and forces her down upon
a dressing room cot.) Now relax—save it. Save everything you've got—you're going to need it.

He leaves her abruptly, exits, and quietly closes the
door.

MARSH (to stagehand; fiercely):
If anyone gets in there—you'll be a corpse!

Stagehand nods and stands arms akimbo outside door,
on guard.

                                      DISSOLVE TO:

342. FULL SHOT   STAGE   BILLY ALONE
as he steps toward footlights for number.

343. FLASH FULL SHOT   ORCHESTRA   SIDE ANGLE
as orchestra leader starts Billy's number.

344. CLOSE SHOT   BILLY
      singing number.

345. CLOSE SHOT   PEGGY IN DRESSING ROOM
      sitting relaxed, eyes closed. At distant sound of Billy's
      number, Peggy opens her eyes, sits up straight, listens,
      smiling happily.

346. CLOSE SHOT   BILLY
      singing his heart out.

347. FULL SHOT   ANGLE
      Billy finishes verse and girl chorus enters.

348. HIGH ANGLE SHOT OF NUMBER
      Billy and girls.

349. MED. SHOT   BILLY AND CHORUS
      as they exit at end of number to hearty applause.
                                              DISSOLVE TO:

350. MED. SHOT   ANDY AND LORRAINE IN WINGS
      Both of them are intently watching Peggy on stage, not
      taking their eyes off her for a single second. Both are
      keyed up and breathless.

      ANDY (through clenched teeth as he flippantly knocks
      Lorraine on the shoulder as one would knock on a door;
      he doesn't look toward her, keeping his eyes on Peggy):
            Do me a favor—will ya?

      LORRAINE (watching Peggy just as intently):
            Not until payday—I won't.

      ANDY:
            I don't mean that. (Tense, as he watches Peggy.) I
            mean—MARRY ME—will ya?

      LORRAINE (still intent on Peggy):
            Well—it's about time. SURE!

ANDY:
Okay then—that's all I wanted to know!

LORRAINE (suspiciously still watching Peggy):
Say—what's the idea?

ANDY (also intent on Peggy; answers out of the side of
his mouth):
It's the only way I know—to keep you away from
me.

DISSOLVE TO:

351.   CLOSE SHOT   MARSH   BACK STAGE
Show nearing its end. Marsh beckons Mac who hurries
to his side.

MARSH (curtly):
Call Sawyer—ready for the finale—

Mac hurries away.

352.   CLOSE SHOT   ORCHESTRA
as leader swings musicians into finale introduction.

353.   MED. SHOT   STAGE DOORMAN'S CHAIR
Abner leans back sound asleep, fatuous smile on face,
the Peke sleeping on his lap. Ann stands beside him,
breathlessly watching the show.

ANN:
Sawyer's a riot—I tell you—she's a riot! Did you
ever—

She suddenly looks at him, notes that he is asleep, and,
hands on hips, is about to bawl him out, when her gaze
fastens on his watch chain. Looking furtively around,
she is about to grab it, when she suddenly notices Lorraine.

ANN (shrugging):
On second thought—what's the use— Eventually
I'll have his socks!

DISSOLVE TO:

354. FULL SHOT   STAGE
     as Peggy and boys start number.

355–357. ALLOWED FOR TRICK SHOTS
     after production number is set. Suggested:
          355: Stage and auditorium as seen from CAMERA at
     back wall of theater, shooting through boys and beyond
     Peggy.
          356: Shot from underneath feet and legs as though
     stage floor were made of plate glass.
          357: Shot Peggy and boys from second balcony.
     Heads of audience in first rows showing and stage with
     proscenium beyond.

358. CLOSE SHOT   PEGGY
     going into tap routine as lights black out, leaving her
     alone in small, circular pool of light.

359–361. ALLOWED FOR TRICK SHOTS
     of Peggy's tap dance.

362. FULL SHOT   STAGE
     as Peggy finishes tap, lights flood up, disclosing whole
     company behind her on stage, joining her in finale tap,
     in the "42nd Street" number![24]

363. FULL SHOT   STAGE
     as male members of company dance forward to then
     back away from Peggy. We see Billy start forward for his
     turn, dancing through lanes of company.

364. CLOSE SHOT   PEGGY AND BILLY
     as they dance together. Their pantomime and significant
     glances tell us better than words that they are in love
     with each other.

365. FULL SHOT   STAGE
     as grinning, ecstatic Billy dances back away from her to

others in company. Lights begin to dim as chorus and principals drift and filter in wings. Finally the stage is dark and empty save for the patch of light in which Peggy is dancing down the curtain.

WIPE OFF TO:

366. EXT. MED. SHOT   SIDE ENTRANCE OF THEATER   NIGHT

Marsh, exhausted, alone, whipped in strength but triumphant in achievement, leans wearily against alley wall. Ushers fling orchestra floor side doors open, and torrent of humanity begins to pour out, hitting against Marsh and flowing around and past him as does a stream around a rock in its bed.

We see couples, old and young, all babbling their reactions to the show. The microphone picks these up here and there.

AD LIBS:

That Sawyer girl was the whole show for me! Those dancers were all right, yes *sir, all right!* Great! Swell! It's a hit! Knockout! Sensational! These directors kill me! Take Marsh; sticks his name all over the program and gets all the credit. Wasn't for kids like Sawyer, he wouldn't have a show. I can't see that Marsh did a thing. It's simply having the right cast—that's all! Sawyer's a whizz. She'll have Broadway in her pocket in a week. Who's this guy Marsh? Anybody could of got a hit with *that* cast and *that* material.

367. CLOSE-UP   MARSH

as he sits on fire escape steps, gloomily sucking cigarette. Last of audience straggles by him. He hears last words:

MAN'S VOICE:

Marsh'll probably claim he discovered her! Some guys get all the breaks!

Marsh flips cigarette into small pool of water in alley, feels unshaven cheeks, and smiles grimly.

MARSH:

Just another show!

He yawns, closes his eyes, leans his head against the fire escape, and goes to sleep.

FADE OUT

THE END

Notes to the Screenplay

1 Jones and Barry were originally Jews whose names were Friedman and Green. In the screenplay before the final, the authors go back and forth between both sets of names. Although the Warner brothers were themselves Jewish, the authors evidently felt it would be safer, at the box office, to use only Anglo-Saxon names. The Bradford Ropes novel has a number of racial slurs. Two examples: "Illiterate Jewish theater owners with no feeling for art except its echo at the box office sought Marsh because of his reputed smartness" and "A worried and unmistakably Semitic voice asked for Mr. Denning." Fortunately Jack Warner (according to his autobiography) only read synopses of the novels the studio purchased—and his brothers didn't even read the synopses.

2 The Depression was totally ignored in the novel and in the earlier screen treatments. Since Warner Brothers was the most socially conscious studio of the thirties and known for its realistic handling of topical material, it was decided that the subject could no longer be ignored, not even in a musical.

3 Abner Dillon was not in the novel; instead a Dick Endicott was *Pretty Lady*'s angel. Endicott was a romantic (though dull) rather than a comic figure (as played by Guy Kibbee). In the earlier treatments, Dillon had earned his millions by raising pigs.

4 This second, more oblique reference to the Depression recalls *Variety*'s oft-quoted headline: Wall Street Lays an Egg.

5 Until the screenplay before the final, Marsh is neither broke nor sick.

6 Mervyn LeRoy, who was assigned to direct *42nd Street* and who was dating Ginger Rogers at the time, suggested that she accept the small but flashy role of Ann ("Anytime Annie") Lowell. Rogers had been in films since 1930 and had played leads in some minor films, but her career was at a standstill. The role of Ann Lowell, LeRoy felt, would lead to stardom for Rogers. He became ill and Bacon took over as director, but Rogers stayed on as Lowell. LeRoy (who later gave Lana Turner her first big break) subsequently cast Rogers in his *Gold Diggers of 1933*. Both films led to her role opposite Fred Astaire in *Flying down to Rio* and to the stardom that had eluded her for several years.

7 Before her role in *42nd Street*, Rogers had played mainly "sweet young things." Her ease at handling such wisecracks at this made casting directors sit up and take notice at last. She is the first to admit that she owes a great deal to Mervyn LeRoy.

8 The writers finally settled on Sioux City, Iowa. Originally Sawyer had come from various "hick" towns in various states (in the novel and in the early treatments she was a New Englander with a broad *a* accent). Presumably, to the authors, Sioux City, Iowa, was the hickest of the hick.

9 In the novel and in the earlier treatments the gangster was a George Raft type—sleek, smooth, and outwardly refined. He owns a speakeasy, he is a bootlegger, and his name is Walt McDermott (admittedly not a George Raft name). Slim Murphy is simply a tough, cheap hood.

10 In the novel he never gets "a sudden attack of manhood." He's on the make and on the take throughout.

11 This song is meant to be bad, of course. But it is *so* bad that it's difficult to believe that a genius-impresario, such as Julian Marsh is supposed to be, would even consider it for *Pretty Lady*.

12 The song is "You're Getting to Be a Habit with Me."

13 In the film Sawyer becomes aware of the relationship between Pat Denning and Dorothy Brock when she sees two photographs of Brock on a table behind the divan.

14 This scene is both more daring and more amusing in the film. Denning carries Sawyer into the bedroom. *We* know that he is too decent a guy to do anything, but she is not so sure as she pleads with him to "please, put me down."

15 In the novel Waring is a prominent character; in the various treatments he is seen less and less; in the movie he disappears entirely.

16 Pages being flipped or torn from a calendar was a common, too obvious device used, in the films of the thirties, to indicate the passage of time. Here, with the dancing feet kicking off the pages, we have the same old device with a new twist. The disorienting jump cut, so common today, was rarely used in the thirties. Few dared to disorient audiences in those days.

17 In the novel and in the earlier treatments, Andy Lee was the dance director. Now he has been demoted to stage manager. MacElroy had been demoted even further: from "book" director of *Pretty Lady* to mere assistant. Julian Marsh was strictly a producer in the novel and in the earlier screen treatments.

18 Known as the actor in the film credits, the old man (played by

Henry B. Walthall) is almost completely out of the movie. If you look quickly, you'll see him in the scene in the theater alley when Sawyer has fainted and Denning has come to her rescue. Though a star in the silent days, Walthall was reduced to playing supporting roles in films with such titles as *Police Court* and *Laughing at Life*.

19 In the film Brock neither throws a Victrola nor falls over one. She simply falls as Denning struggles to calm her. The idea of Brock's throwing a Victrola was perhaps thought ludicrous—or, to the Warner studio, wasteful.

20 Marsh's streak of cruelty, more pronounced in the novel, is not in the film.

21 One of the major weaknesses of both the script and the movie is that we are not prepared for Ann Lowell's big self-sacrificing scene. We do not know Lowell well enough to convince us that she is capable of this selfless act, nor do we ever see the talent that Sawyer supposedly possesses. Ironically enough, Ginger Rogers (Ann Lowell) later in the year (*Flying down to Rio*) proved to be a better singer, dancer, and actress than Keeler.

22 Thanks to trouper Bebe Daniels as Dorothy Brock, this speech is not quite as corny as it reads on paper.

23 This is the first time this famous line ("You're going out a youngster—you've *got* to come back a star!") appears in any of the scripts. It was not in the novel, either. It never fails to move students to a combination of jeers and cheers—and it's the one line in the movie they never forget.

24 Outside of the "It Must Be June" nonsense, this is the only production number that is identified in the script by name. The number is not mentioned in any of the earlier treatments. Of the other production numbers, "Shuffle off to Buffalo" begins at scene 333 of the screenplay and "Young and Healthy" begins at scene 343.

Production Credits

Directed by	Lloyd Bacon
Dances and ensembles created and staged by	Busby Berkeley
*Words and music by**	Al Dubin and Harry Warren
Screenplay by	Rian James and James Seymour
Based on the novel by	Bradford Ropes
Edited by	Frank Ware and Thomas Pratt
Art Director	Jack Okey
Photography by	Sol Polito
Gowns by	Orry-Kelly
Silks by	Cheney Brothers
Vitaphone Orchestra conducted by	Leo F. Forbstein

Released: March 1933
Running time: 89 minutes

*"42nd Street," "Shuffle off to Buffalo," "You're Getting to Be a Habit with Me," "Young and Healthy"

Cast

Julian Marsh	Warner Baxter
Dorothy Brock	Bebe Daniels
Pat Denning	George Brent
Peggy Sawyer	Ruby Keeler
Abner Dillon	Guy Kibbee
Lorraine Fleming	Una Merkel
Ann ("Anytime Annie") Lowell	Ginger Rogers
Thomas Barry	Ned Sparks
Billy Lawler	Dick Powell
MacElroy	Allen Jenkins
Terry Neil	Eddie Nugent
Al Jones	Robert McWade
Andy Lee	George E. Stone
Jerry	Harry Akst
"Shuffle off to Buffalo" groom	Clarence Nordstrom
Old actor	Henry B. Walthall
Songwriters	Al Dubin
	Harry Warren
"Young and Healthy" girl	Toby Wing

Inventory

The following materials from the Warner library of the Wisconsin Center for Film and Theater Research were used by Fumento in preparing *42nd Street* for the Wisconsin/Warner Bros. Screenplay Series:

Novel (typescript), by Bradford Ropes, August 10, 1932, 378 pages.
Treatment, by Whitney Bolton, August 16, 1932, 38 pages.
Treatment, by Bolton and James Seymour, August 22, 1932, 22 pages.
Temporary, by Bolton and Seymour, September 8, 1932, 198 pages.
Revised Temporary, by Seymour and Bolton, September 16, 1932, 152 pages.
Final, [by Rian James and James Seymour], no date, 156 pages.

DESIGNED BY GARY GORE
COMPOSED BY THE NORTH CENTRAL PUBLISHING CO.
ST. PAUL, MINNESOTA
MANUFACTURED BY INTER-COLLEGIATE PRESS, INC.
SHAWNEE MISSION, KANSAS
TEXT AND DISPLAY LINES ARE SET IN PALATINO

Library of Congress Cataloging in Publication Data
James, Rian, 1899–
42nd Street.
(Wisconsin/Warner Bros. screenplay series)
Screenplay, by R. James and J. Seymour,
for the motion picture 42nd Street, based on the novel by B. Ropes.
I. Seymour, James, joint author.
II. Fumento, Rocco, 1923–
III. Ropes, Bradford. 42nd Street.
IV. Wisconsin Center for Film and Theater Research.
V. 42nd Street. [Motion picture] VI. Series.
PN1997.F596   812'.52   80-5106
ISBN 0-299-08100-1
ISBN 0-299-08104-4 (pbk.)

WW
WISCONSIN/WARNER BROS SCREENPLAY SERIES

The Wisconsin/Warner Bros. Screenplay Series, a product of the Warner Brothers Film Library, will enable film scholars, students, researchers, and aficionados to gain insights into individual American films in ways never before possible.

The Warner library was acquired in 1957 by the United Artists Corporation, which in turn donated it to the Wisconsin Center for Film and Theater Research in 1969. The massive library, housed in the State Historical Society of Wisconsin, contains eight hundred sound feature films, fifteen hundred short subjects, and nineteen thousand still negatives, as well as the legal files, press books, and screenplays of virtually every Warner film produced from 1930 until 1950. This rich treasure trove has made the University of Wisconsin one of the major centers for film research, attracting scholars from around the world. This series of published screenplays represents a creative use of the Warner library, both a boon to scholars and a tribute to United Artists.

Most published film scripts are literal transcriptions of finished films. The Wisconsin/Warner screenplays are primary source documents—the final shooting versions including revisions made during production. As such, they will explicate the art of screenwriting as film transcriptions cannot. They will help the user to understand the arts of directing and acting, as well as the other arts involved in the film-making process, in comparing these screenplays with the final films. (Films of the Warner library are available at modest rates from the United Artists nontheatrical rental library, United Artists/16 mm.)

From the eight hundred feature films in the library, the general editor and the editorial committee of the series have chosen those that have received critical recognition for their excellence of directing, screenwriting, and acting, films that are distinctive examples of their genre, those that have particular historical relevance, and some that are adaptations of well-known novels and plays. The researcher, instructor, or student can, in the judicious selection of individual volumes for close examination, gain a heightened appreciation and broad understanding of the American film and its historical role during this critical period.